Listening
TO THE
Great Teacher

"Let the young children come to me,
and do not try to stop them."
—Luke 18:16.

CONTENTS

CONTENTS

NOTE: The scriptures referred to in this book may be found in any translation of the Bible. However, unless otherwise indicated, direct quotations are from the modern-language "New World Translation of the Holy Scriptures." Citations marked "Dy" show where the same information is found in the Catholic "Douay Version."

A Word to You Parents

The love of parents for their children is a wonderful quality. Like most parents, you are undoubtedly concerned with giving your children a good start in life.

But we are sure you realize that there is more to this than simply providing food and clothing for your children and sending them off to school to be educated. To face life successfully, children need moral guidance, principles by which to live. And they need these from their tender years on. Heartbreaking things can and do happen where children receive help too late.

Perhaps, like many parents, you feel somewhat at a loss as to where to begin and what to teach your children. Really, the best principles that can be found anywhere are found in the Bible. Instruction based on the Bible has definite advantages. By it, children come to realize that what they are being told is not just their father's or mother's idea. It is what their Creator says; it is his will. This gives a strength to parental counsel that cannot be equaled in any other way.

In the pages of the Bible God encourages parents to take a personal interest in impressing right principles on the minds of their children. It may seem easier to pass this responsibility on to someone else. But doing that means missing out on a very enriching experience. It means giving up the opportunity to reach your child's heart in a way that you and no one else ever could.

In many homes today parents and children are steadily drifting apart. As children grow older, parents often find it increasingly hard to talk with them about things that matter the most. This book, "Listening to the Great Teacher," is designed to help to prevent such a situation in your home. It is designed so that you and your children can read it together. But, more than this, it is designed to stimulate conversation between parents and children.

This is because it calls for a response on the part of the children. You will find many well-placed questions in the printed material. When you come to these, you will observe a dash (—), to remind you to pause and encourage your child to express himself. Children like to be involved. Without that involvement a child's interest quickly fades. More importantly, though, these questions will help you to learn what is on your child's mind. Of course, the child may come out with answers that are far from right. But the printed material that follows each question is designed to help the child to develop wholesome patterns of thinking.

When the child learns to read, encourage him to read the book to you, and at times to himself. The more he reads it, the more its good counsel will be impressed on his mind and heart. But, to strengthen the bonds of affection and respect between both of you parents and your child, by all means read the book together, and do it regularly.

Some Bible texts are cited at the end of each chapter. Why not take time to look these up together? You and your children can thereby learn to use the Bible well. Explain what these scriptures are saying. Help make clear any difficult words in the scriptures that you look up, as is done in this book. Doing this, you will be directing your child's attention to the finest source of guidance in life, the Bible.

We sincerely hope this book will help you and your family to mold your lives so as to be pleasing to the Creator, to your eternal blessing.

—THE PUBLISHERS

1

Jesus, the Great Teacher

DO YOU like to hear stories? — Well, then, I'm going to tell you one about a man who told better stories than anyone else who has ever lived on earth. His name is Jesus Christ.

He lived on this earth almost two thousand years ago. That is a long time ago. It is long before your grandmother or grandfather were born. And it is long before men had cars or trains or radios or other things of today.

When Jesus told a story it made a person think. If a person thought about it long enough, what Jesus said could even change the way the person felt about things. It could change the person's whole view of life. And everything that Jesus said was true.

Jesus knew more than any other man. He was the best teacher who ever lived. We learn many things from other persons. But we can learn the most important things from Jesus.

One reason that Jesus was such a great teacher is because he listened. He knew how important it is to listen. But to whom did Jesus listen? Who taught him? — Jesus' Father did. And Jesus' Father is God.

Before coming to earth as a man, Jesus had lived in heaven with God. So Jesus was different from other men. For no other man lived in heaven before being born on earth. In heaven Jesus had been a good Son who listened to his Father. So Jesus was able to teach people what he learned from God. By listening to your father and mother you can copy Jesus.

Another reason why Jesus was a great teacher is that he loved people. He wanted to help them to learn about God.
Jesus loved grown-ups. But did he love children too? — Yes, he did. And children liked to be with Jesus because he would talk to them and listen to them.

One day parents brought their young children to Jesus. But Jesus' friends thought that the Great Teacher was too busy to speak with little children. So they told them to go away. But did Jesus agree? — No. He said: 'Let the young children alone, and do not stop them from coming to me.' Even though he was a very wise and important man, Jesus took time to teach little children.—Matthew 19:13, 14.

Jesus was a great teacher because he knew how to make things interesting. He spoke about birds and flowers and other things to help people understand about God. One day he gave a sermon or a talk to a large crowd of people who came to him when he was on the side of a mountain. It is called the Sermon on the Mount.

Jesus told the people: 'Look at the birds in the sky. They do not plant seed. They do not store food in houses. But God in heaven feeds them. Are you not worth more than they are?'

Jesus also said: 'Take a lesson from the lilies of the field.' What lesson do you think we can learn from them? Well, Jesus said: 'They do not make clothes. And look how beautiful they are! Even rich King Solomon was not dressed more beautifully than the lilies of the field. So if God takes care of the flowers that grow, will he not also care for you?'

Do you understand the lesson Jesus was teaching there? — He did not want them to worry about where they would get food to eat or

clothes to put on. God knows that people need these things. Jesus did not say that we should not work for food and clothing. But he said that we should put God first. If we do that, God will see that we have food to eat and clothing to wear. Do you believe that? — —Matthew 6:25-33.

People liked the way Jesus taught. They were amazed. It was interesting to listen to him. And what he said helped people to do what is right.

It is important that we listen to him too. But how can we do that? We have the sayings of Jesus written in a book. Do you know what that book is? — It is the Holy Bible. So we can listen to Jesus by paying attention to the Bible.

God himself says that we should listen to Jesus. One day when Jesus was with three of his friends up in a high mountain, a voice from heaven said: "This is my Son, the beloved, whom I have approved; listen to him." Do you know whose voice that was? — It was God's! God said that we should listen to his Son.—Matthew 17:1-5.

Will you listen to the Great Teacher? — That is what we all should do. We will be happy if we do. And it will also bring us happiness if we tell our friends the good things we learn.

(For more fine thoughts about the benefits that come from listening to Jesus, open your Bible and read together John 8:28-30; 3:16; Acts 4:12.)

2

A Letter from God

TELL me, which book do you like best of all? —
Some children would pick one that tells about
animals. Others would choose a book with lots
of pictures in it. It can be fun to read those
books.

But the best books in all the world are the
ones that tell us the truth about God. And one
of those books is more precious than all the
others. Do you know which one it is? — The
Bible.

Why is the Bible so important? — Because it
came from God. It tells us about him and about
the good things that he will do for us. And it
shows us what we should do in order to please
him. It is like a letter from God.

Now, God could have written the whole Bible
in heaven and then given it to man. But he
didn't. The ideas came from God. But he used
his servants on earth to do most of the writing.

How did he do that? — An example can help
us to understand. When people hear a voice on
the radio it is from someone far away. They
cannot see him, but they can hear what he says,
can't they?

Men can even go all the way to the moon in
their spaceships, and they can send messages

back to the earth from there. Did you know that? — If men can do that, can God send messages from heaven? — Of course he can! And he did it long before men had radio and television.

Moses was one man to whom God spoke. Moses could not see God, but he could hear the voice. Millions of people were there when this happened. They saw it when God caused a whole mountain to shake, and there was thunder and lightning. They heard it when a voice came from heaven. They knew that God had spoken. God spoke to Moses again later on, and Moses wrote down the things that God said. What he wrote is in the Bible.—Exodus 19:3–20:21.

It was not only Moses that wrote. God used about forty men to write parts of the Bible. They wrote down things that God was going to do in the future. How did they know those things before they even happened? — God had talked to them.

By the time that Jesus, the Great Teacher, was on earth, a big part of the Bible had been written. Now, remember, the Great Teacher had been in heaven. He knew what God had done. Did he believe that the Bible was from God? — Yes, he did.

When Jesus talked to people about the works of God, he read from the Bible. Sometimes he told them from memory what it said.

Jesus also brought us more information from

God. He said: 'The very things I heard from God I am speaking in the world.' Jesus had heard many things from God because he had lived with God. And where can we read those things that Jesus said? — In the Bible. It was all written down for us to read.—John 8:26.

Of course, when God used men to write, they wrote in the language that they used every day. So part of the Bible was written in Hebrew, some in Aramaic, and quite a bit in Greek. Most people today do not know how to read those languages. Do you? —

That is why the Bible has been copied into other languages. Today there are parts of the Bible in over one thousand four hundred languages. Just think of that! The Bible is God's letter to people everywhere. So it has to be in

many languages. But no matter how many times it has been copied, the message is from God.

What the Bible says is important for us. It was written a long time ago. But it tells about things that are happening to-day. And it tells us what God is going to do in the near future. What it says is exciting! It gives us a wonderful hope.

The Bible also tells us how God wants us to live. It tells us what is right and what is wrong. You need to know this and so do I. It tells us about people who did bad things, and what happened to them. So we can avoid the trouble they had. It also tells us about people who did right, and the good results that came to them. It was all written down for our good.

But to get the most out of the Bible, we need to know the answer to a question. The question is this: "Who gave us the Bible?" What would you say? — Yes, all of it is from God.

But some people do not listen to what God says in the Bible. They just live the way they want to. Do you think that is right? — Do you think that anyone knows more than God does? — The way to show that we are really wise is to listen to God. And then we ought to do what he says.

So we need to take time to read the Bible together. When we get a letter from someone that we love very much, we read it again and again. It is precious to us. That is the way the Bible should be to us, because it is a letter from the One who loves us most. It is a letter from God.

(Take a few more minutes now and read these scriptures that show that the Bible truly is God's Word, written for our benefit: 2 Timothy 3:16, 17; 2 Peter 1:20, 21; Romans 15:4.)

3

The One Who Made All Things

I KNOW something wonderful. Would you like to hear it? — Look at your hand. Bend your fingers. Now pick something up. Your hand can do many things, and it can do them well. Do you know who made the hand? — It was God.

Now look at my face. What do you see? — You see my mouth, my nose and my two eyes. How can you see them? — With your own eyes. And who made the eyes? — It was God. Isn't that wonderful? —

You can see many things with your eyes. You can look at flowers. You can see birds. You can look at the green grass and the blue sky.

But who made these things? — Did some man make them? — No. Men can make a house. But no man can make grass that grows. Men cannot make a bird, a flower or any other living thing. Did you know that? —

God is the One who made all these things. God made the heavens and the earth. He made people too. He created the first man and the first woman. Jesus, the Great Teacher, taught this.—Matthew 19:4-6.

How did Jesus know that God made man and woman? Did Jesus see God do it? — Yes, he did. Jesus was with God when God made man and woman. Jesus was the first person that God made. He was an angel, and he lived and worked in heaven with his Father.

The Bible tells us that God said: "Let us make man." Do you know whom God was talking to? — He was talking to his Son, the one who later came to earth and became the Great Teacher!—Genesis 1:26.

Everything that God has done shows his love. God made the sun. The sun gives us light and it keeps us warm. Everything would be cold and there would be no life on earth if we did not have the sun. Aren't you glad that God made the sun? —

God makes it rain too. Sometimes you may not like the rain because you can't go outside to play when it rains. But the rain helps the flowers to grow.

So when we see beautiful flowers, whom are we going to thank for them? — God. And whom should we thank when we eat fruits and vegetables that taste good? — We should thank God, because it is his sun and rain that make

16

things grow. God is so good to do all these wonderful things for us.

Do you know where God is? — The Bible tells us that God lives in heaven.

Can you see God? — No. The Bible says: 'No man can see God.' So no one should try to make a picture or an image of God. God even tells us not to try to make an image of him. So we should not have things like those in our house, should we? — —Exodus 33:20; 20:4, 5.

But if you cannot see God, how do you know that there really is a God? — Think about this. Can you see the wind? — No. Nobody can see the wind. But you can see the things the wind does. You can see the leaves move when the wind blows through the branches of a tree. So you believe that there is wind.

You can see the things God has done too. When you see a living flower or a bird, you see something God has made. So you believe that there really is a God.

Someone might ask you, "Who made the sun and the earth?" What would you say? — You can say that God made them. The Bible says: "God created the heavens and the earth." —Genesis 1:1.

What if someone asks you, "Did God make man and the animals too?" What will you say? — Tell him: "Yes, God made man and the animals. God made the birds too." The Bible says: 'God created all things.'—Ephesians 3:9.

Someone may tell you that he does not believe in God. What will you say then? — Why not point to a house? Ask the person: "Who made that house?" Some man did. The house did not make itself, did it? —

Then take the person to a garden and show him a flower. Ask him: "Who made this?" No man did. Since the house did not make itself, this flower did not make itself. Someone made it. God did.

Ask the person to stop and listen to the song of a bird. Then ask him: "Who made the birds and taught them to sing?" God did. God is the One who made the heavens and the earth and all living things! He is the One who gives life.

And how good it is to be alive! We can hear the beautiful songs of the birds. We can see the flowers and the other things that God has made. And we can eat the foods that God has given us.

For all these things we should thank God. Most of all, we should thank him for giving us life. If we are really thankful to God, we will do something. What is that? — We will listen to God and we will worship him in the way that he tells us to in the Bible. In that way we can show that we love the One who made all things.

(We should show appreciation to God for all that he has done. How? Read what is written at Psalm 139:14 [138:14, Douay Version], Revelation 4:11, John 4:23, 24 and 1 John 5:21.)

4

God Has a Name

WHAT is your name? — You have a name. So do I. The first man on earth had a name. God called him Adam. The first woman was named Eve. Every man, woman and child has a name.

Look up at the many, many stars at night. Do you think they have names? — Yes, God gave a name to each star in the sky. The Bible tells us: "He is counting the number of the stars; all of them he calls by their names."—Psalm 147:4.

People and stars all have names. So do you think that God has a name? — The Great Teacher said that he does. He once said in prayer to God: 'I have made your name known to my followers.'—John 17:26.

Do you know God's name? — God himself tells us what it is. He says: "I am Jehovah. That is my name." So God's name is JEHOVAH. —Isaiah 42:8.

Do you like it when others remember your name? — People like to be called by their name. And Jehovah wants people to know his name too. So we should use the name Jehovah when we talk about God.

The Great Teacher used God's name Jehovah when he spoke to people. One time he said:

"You must love Jehovah your God with your whole heart."—Mark 12:30.

Jesus knew that "Jehovah" is a very important name. So he taught his followers to use God's name. He even taught them to speak about God's name in their prayers.

Long ago God showed the importance of his name to the man Moses. Moses was one of the sons of Israel. The sons of Israel lived in a land called Egypt. The Egyptians made the sons of Israel slaves and were very mean to them. When Moses grew up, he tried to help one of his people. This made the king of Egypt angry. He wanted to kill Moses! So Moses ran away from Egypt.

Moses went to another land. It was the land of Midian. There he worked as a shepherd, taking care of sheep. One day he saw an amazing thing. A thornbush was on fire, but it was not burning up! Moses went closer to take a better look.

Do you know what happened? — Moses heard a voice from the middle of that burning bush. The voice called, "Moses! Moses!"

Who was saying that? — It was God speaking! God had a big work for Moses to do. God said: 'Come and let me send you to Pharaoh, the king of Egypt, and you bring my people the sons of Israel out of Egypt.' God promised to help Moses.

But Moses said to God: 'Suppose I come to the sons of Israel in Egypt and say to them that God sent me. What if they ask me, What is his name? What shall I say?' God told Moses to tell the sons of Israel: 'Jehovah has sent me to you. Jehovah is my name forever.'—Exodus 3:1-15.

This shows that God was going to keep the name Jehovah. God wanted to be known by the name Jehovah forever.

Moses went back to Egypt. The Egyptians there did not really know Jehovah. They thought that he was just a small god of the sons of Israel. The Egyptians did not think that Jehovah was the God of the whole earth. So Jehovah told the king of Egypt: 'I am going to make my name known in all the earth.'—Exodus 9:16.

Jehovah did make his name known in all the earth. He had

Moses lead the sons of Israel out of Egypt. And people in all the earth soon heard about Jehovah.

Today many people are just as those Egyptians were. They do not believe that Jehovah is the God of the whole earth.

So Jehovah wants his people to tell others about him. This is what Jesus did.

Do you want to be like Jesus? — Then tell others that God's name is Jehovah. You will find that many persons do not know that. So perhaps you can show them the scripture in the Bible at Psalm 83:18. Let's get the Bible right now and find that scripture together. It says: "That people may know that you, whose name is Jehovah, you alone are the Most High over all the earth."

"Jehovah" is the most important name there is. It is the name of the One who made all things. And remember, Jesus said that we should love Jehovah with our whole heart. Do you love Jehovah? —

How can we show that we love him? — One way is to tell others his name Jehovah. We can also tell them about the wonderful things that he has done. This will please Jehovah, because he knows that people need to know about him. We can have a share in doing that, can't we? —

Not everyone will want to listen when we speak about Jehovah. Many people did not listen even when Jesus talked about Him. But that did not stop Jesus from speaking about Jehovah.

So let's be like Jesus. Let's keep talking about Jehovah. If we do, Jehovah God will be pleased with us because we show love for his name.

(Now read together from the Bible a few more texts showing the importance of God's name: John 17:26; Isaiah 12:4, 5; Romans 10:13.)

5

"This Is My Son"

EVERYONE has a father. You have a father. And I have a father. When a girl does good things, her father is pleased to tell others: "This is my daughter." And when a boy does what is right, his father is proud to say: "This is my son."

Jesus always does what pleases his Father. So his Father feels pleased with him. And do you know what Jesus' Father did? — He spoke all the way from heaven to tell men: "This is my Son."

Jesus really loves his Father. He showed this even before he came to the earth. He had a wonderful place in heaven with his Father, Jehovah God. But God had a special work for Jesus to do. To do that work, Jesus had to leave heaven. He had to be born as a baby on earth. Jesus was willing to do this because Jehovah wanted him to do it.

To be born as a baby on earth, Jesus had to have a mother. Do you know who she was? — Her name was Mary.

Jehovah sent his angel Gabriel from heaven to talk to Mary. Gabriel told Mary she was going to have a baby boy. The baby would be named Jesus. And who would the baby's father be? — The angel said that the baby's father would be Jehovah God. That is why Jesus would be called the Son of God.

How do you think Mary felt about this? — Did she say, 'I don't want to do that'? Did she say, 'I don't want to be the mother of Jesus'? —

No, Mary was ready to do what God wanted. She was very willing to listen to God's angel. It was like listening to God! And Mary wanted to listen to God. She loved God and was glad to do what Jehovah God wanted her to do.

But how could Jehovah cause his Son in heaven to be born as a baby on earth? — Jehovah is the most powerful one anywhere. He can do things no one else can do. So Jehovah took the life of his Son from heaven and put it inside Mary. Jesus began to grow inside of Mary just as other babies grow inside of their mothers. After that Mary married Joseph.

Then the time came for Jesus to be born. He was born in the city of Bethlehem. Mary and her husband Joseph were visiting that city. But Bethlehem was full of people. There was not even a room where Mary and Joseph could stay on the night that Jesus was born. They had to put the baby Jesus in a manger. A manger is a place that holds food for cows and other animals to eat.

Exciting things happened on the night that Jesus was born. Near Bethlehem an angel talked to some shepherds. He told the shepherds what an important person Jesus was. He said to

them: 'Look! I am telling you good news that will make people happy. To-day someone was born who will save the people.' Jesus would do many good things for people who love God.—Luke 2:10, 11.

This was good news! Other angels in heaven began to join together in praising God. They were happy! The shepherds could hear what they said.

Now the shepherds wanted to see Jesus. The angel told them that they could find Jesus in Bethlehem. So they went there. When the shepherds got there to see Jesus, they told Joseph and Mary all the good things they had heard. This made Joseph and Mary very thankful to God. Can you imagine how happy Mary was that she had been willing to be the mother of Jesus?

Later, Joseph and Mary took Jesus to the city of Nazareth. That is where Jesus grew up. When he was grown, he began his great teaching work. This was part of the work Jehovah God wanted his Son to do on earth.

About three years later, Jesus and some of his followers went up on a high mountain. What happened there? — As the others watched, Jesus' clothes began to shine brightly. Then God's own voice was heard. Jehovah said about Jesus: "This is my Son, the beloved." God was pleased with his Son.—Mark 9:2-8.

Jesus always did what was right. He did not pretend to be someone that he really was not. He did not tell people that he was God. The angel Gabriel had told Mary that Jesus would be called the Son of God. Jesus himself said that he is God's Son. And he did not tell people that he knew more than his Father. He said: "The Father is greater than I am."—John 14:28.

When Jesus' Father gave him work to do, Jesus did it. He did not say, 'Yes, I will do it,' but then do something else. He loved his Father. So he listened to what his Father said.

We want to please Jehovah too, don't we? — Then we must show that we really listen to God, as Jesus did. God speaks to us through the Bible. It would not be right to pretend to listen to God, but then believe and do things that are contrary to the Bible, would it? — And remember, we won't find it hard to please Jehovah if we really love him.

(Other texts showing why we need to know and believe what the Bible really says about Jesus: Matthew 7:21-23, 1 Timothy 2:5, 6 and John 4:25, 26.)

6

The Great Teacher Served Other People

DO YOU like it when someone does something for you? — Well, other people like it when someone does something for them too. We all do. The Great Teacher knew that, and he was always doing things for people. He said: 'I came, not to be served, but to serve.'—Matthew 20:28.

So, if we want to be like the Great Teacher, what must we do? — We must serve others. We must do good things for them.

It is true, many people do not do this. In fact, most people always want others to serve them. At one time even Jesus' followers felt this way. Each one wanted to be the most important.

Jesus knew that it was not right for them to think this way. So, one day he gave them a lesson that they would never forget.

While they were having a meal together, Jesus got up from the table. He took a washbasin and put water into it. As they watched, Jesus went around to each one of them, bent down and washed their feet. Then he dried their feet with a towel. Just think of that! What if you had been there and Jesus had washed your feet? How would you have felt? —

His followers did not feel it was right for the Great Teacher to serve them in this way. They felt embarrassed. In fact, one of them was not going to let Jesus do this lowly service for him. But Jesus said that it was important for him to do it.

We do not usually wash one another's feet today. But it was common to do it when Jesus was on earth. Do you know why? —

Well, in the land where they lived, people wore open sandals on their bare feet. So when they walked on the dirt roads, their feet got covered with dust. It was a kindness to wash the dusty feet of a person who came into the house to visit. But this time not

one of Jesus' followers offered to wash the feet of the others. So Jesus did it himself. By doing this, Jesus taught his followers an important lesson. They needed to learn this lesson. And it is a lesson that we today need to learn.

Do you know what that lesson is? — After Jesus took his place at the table again, he explained: 'Do you understand what I did to you? You call me "Teacher" and "Lord," and you are right. If I, your Teacher and Lord, washed your feet, then you should wash the feet of one another.'—John 13:2-14.

Here the Great Teacher showed that he wanted his followers to serve one another. He did not want them to think only about themselves. He did not want them to think that they were so important that others should always serve them. He wanted them to be willing to serve others.

Wasn't that a fine lesson? — Will you be like the Great Teacher and serve other people? — We can all do things for others.

It is not hard to serve other people. If you watch, you will find many things that you can do for other persons.

Think now: Is there anything you can do to help your mother? You know that she does many things for you and the rest of the family. Can you help her? — Why not ask her? —

Maybe you can set the table before the family eats. Or maybe you can stack the dirty

29

dishes after the family finishes eating. Some children take the garbage out every day. Whatever it is you can do, it will be serving others, even as Jesus did.

Do you have younger brothers and sisters that you can serve? — Remember, Jesus, the Great Teacher, served even his followers. By serving your younger brothers and sisters, you will be copying Jesus.

What can you do for them? Can you think of anything? — Maybe you can help them to learn to put their toys away when they are finished playing. Or maybe you can help them to get ready for bed. They will come to love you for doing these things, just as Jesus' followers loved him.

In school, too, you can serve other people. If someone drops his books, it would be kind of you to help him to pick them up. You might offer to clean the blackboard for your teacher, or to do something else for her. Even holding the door open for someone is a kind service.

At times we will find that people will not thank us for serving them. Do you think this should stop us from doing good? — No! Many people did not thank Jesus for his good works. But that did not stop him from doing good.

So let's never hold back from serving people. Let's always follow the example of Jesus.

(For more scriptures about helping other people, read Romans 15:1, 2, Proverbs 3:27, 28 and Galatians 6:2.)

7

Obedience Protects You

WOULD you like it if you could do anything you wanted? Are there times when you wish that no one would ever tell you what to do? Now, be honest and tell me. —

But which is better for you? Is it really wise to do anything you want? Or do things turn out better when you obey your father and your mother? — God says that you should obey your parents, so there must be a good reason for it. Let's see if we can figure it out.

How old are you? — Do you know how old your father is? — How old is your mother? — They have lived much longer than you have. And the longer a person lives the more time he has to learn things. He hears more things, and sees more things and does more things every year. So young folks can learn from older ones.

Who has lived longer than you or I or any other person? — Jehovah God has. He knows more than you do and he knows more than I do. When he tells us what is good for us, we can be sure that it is right. If we do what he says, it will protect us. We should always obey him.

So you see, I need to be obedient too. I need to obey God. It is for my own good. And it brings good to you too when you obey God.

Let's get out our Bible and see what God tells children to do. Can you find the book of Ephesians? — We are going to read from Ephesians chapter six, verses one, two and three. It says: "Children, be obedient to your parents in union with the Lord, for this is righteous: 'Honor your father and your mother'; which is the first command with a promise: 'That it may go well with you and you may endure a long time on the earth.'"

That is in the Bible. So it is Jehovah God who is telling you to be obedient to your parents.

What does it mean to "honor" your father and your mother? — It means that you are to show them respect. You should listen to them and do what they say without complaining. And God promises that if you obey, it will "go well with you."

I know a story about some people whose lives were saved because they were obedient. Would you like to hear it? —

These people lived in the big city of Jerusalem long ago. Most of the people in that city were bad. They did not listen to God. Jehovah sent his own Son to teach them. But they still did not listen. What would God do to them? —

The Great Teacher warned them that God was going to have their city destroyed. He said that armies of soldiers would camp around the city and ruin it. He also told the people how they could escape if they loved what was right. This is what he said:

'When you see armies all around Jerusalem, then is the time to get out of Jerusalem and run to the mountains.'—Luke 21:20-22.

It happened just as Jesus said it would. The armies of Rome came to attack Jerusalem. They camped all around. Then for some reason they left. Most of the people thought that the danger was past. They stayed in the city. But what had Jesus said they should do? —

What would you have done if you had been living in Jerusalem? — Those who really believed Jesus left their homes and ran far away from Jerusalem into the mountains. Not only grown-ups went; children went with them.

But were they really protected because they were obedient? — For a whole year nothing happened to Jerusalem. For three years nothing happened. But then in the fourth year the armies of Rome came back. For those who had stayed in Jerusalem it was now too late to escape. This time the armies destroyed the city. Most of the people inside were killed.

But what happened to those who had obeyed Jesus? — They were far away from Jerusalem. So they were not hurt. Obedience protected them.

If you are obedient, will that protect you too? — Yes. Let me show you how. I may tell you never to play in the street. Why do I do that? — It is because you might be hit by a car and get killed. But someday you might think: "There are no cars right now. I won't get hurt. Other children play in the street, and I have never seen them get hurt."

That is how most of the people in Jerusalem thought. After the armies of Rome had left, it looked safe. Others were staying in the city. So they stayed too. They had been warned, but they did not listen. As a result, they lost their lives. And children who play in the street can lose their lives too. How much better it is to obey!

Obeying just some of the time is not enough. But if you always obey, it really will protect you.

Who is it that tells you, "Be obedient to your parents"? — It is God. And, remember, he says that because he really loves you.

(Here are some more fine scriptures showing the importance of obedience: Ecclesiastes 12:13; Colossians 3:20; Proverbs 23:22.)

34

8

A Good Neighbor

DO YOU know anyone who has a skin color different from yours? — In some places the skin color of most people is black or brown. In other places almost everyone has white skin. They are born that way.

Does it make you better than other people if you have a different skin color than they do? — Should a person with black skin think that he is better than someone whose skin is white? Or should someone with white skin think he is better than a person whose skin is black? What do you think? —

If we listen to the Great Teacher, Jesus Christ, we will be kind to everyone. It does not make any difference what nation a person may come from or what his skin color is. We ought to love people of all kinds. This is what Jesus taught.

One day a Jew came to ask Jesus a hard question. This man thought Jesus would not know the answer. He said: 'What must I do to live forever?'

This was an easy question for the Great Teacher. But instead of answering it himself, Jesus asked the man: 'What does God's law say we must do?'

The man answered: 'The law of God says,

35

"You must love Jehovah your God with all your heart, and you must love your neighbor as yourself." '

Jesus said: 'You answered right. Keep on doing this and you will get eternal life.'

But the man did not want to love everyone. So he tried to find an excuse. He asked Jesus: "Who really is my neighbor?" How would you have answered that? Who really is your neighbor? —

This man may have wanted Jesus to say: 'Your neighbors are your friends.' But what about other people? Are they our neighbors too? —

To answer the question, Jesus told a story. It was about a Jew and a Samaritan. This is how it went:

A man was going down the road from the city of Jerusalem to Jericho. This man was a Jew. As he was walking along, robbers grabbed him. They knocked him down, and took his money and his clothes. The robbers beat him up and left him beside the road half-dead.

A short time later a priest came along that road. He saw the man who was badly hurt. What did he do? What would you have done? —

The priest just went over to the other side of the road. He did not even stop. He did not do anything at all to help the man.

Then another very religious man came down

the road. He was a Levite, who served in the temple at Jerusalem. Would he stop to help? He did the very same thing as the priest. He offered no help. Was that the right thing to do? —

Finally a Samaritan came along the road. He saw the Jew lying there badly hurt. Now, most Samaritans and Jews did not like each other. So would this Samaritan leave the man without helping him? Would he say to himself: 'Why should I help this Jew? He would not help me if I were hurt'?

Well, this Samaritan looked at the man lying beside the road, and he felt very sorry for him. He could not leave him and let him die.

So the Samaritan got off his animal. He went over to the man, and began caring for his wounds. He poured oil and wine upon them. This would help the wounds to heal. Then he wrapped up the wounds with a cloth.

The Samaritan gently lifted the hurt man up on his animal. Then they went slowly on down the road until they came to an inn, or a small hotel. Here the Samaritan got a place for the man to stay, and he took good care of him.

Now Jesus asked the man to whom he was

talking: 'Which one of these three men do you think was the good neighbor?' How would you answer? Was it the priest, the Levite or the Samaritan? —

The man answered: 'The Samaritan was the good neighbor. He stopped and took care of the hurt man.'

Jesus said: 'You are right. So go your way and do the same yourself.'—Luke 10:25-37.

Wasn't that a fine story? — It makes clear who our neighbors are. Our neighbors are not only our close friends. Our neighbors are not only persons of our own country, or persons who have the same skin color as we do. Our neighbors are people of all kinds.

So if you see someone hurt, what will you do? — What if the person is from a different country or has a skin color different from yours? — He is still your neighbor. So you should help him. If you feel too small to help, then you can ask me to help. Or you can call a policeman, or a schoolteacher. That is being like the Samaritan man.

The Great Teacher wants us to be kind. He wants us to help others, no matter who they may be. That is why he told the story about the man who was a good neighbor.

(On this matter of how we should view people of other races and nations, also read Acts 10:34, 35; 17:26; Matthew 5:44-48.)

9

There Is Someone Higher

HAVE you ever heard anyone say, "I wish I were a grown-up so I could do anything I wanted"? — Have you ever wished that? —

It is true that grown-ups can do some things that children cannot. But none of us can make all our own rules for life. There is someone higher than we are. Do you know who that is? —

Most people agree that God is certainly higher than we are. But it is not enough to say it. We have to prove we believe it by the things that we do.

This is shown by what happened to Adam and Eve. They were the first man and woman. Some people say that the story about Adam and Eve is only make-believe. But the Great Teacher did not say that. He knew that it was true. Listen, and I will tell you what happened.

When God made Adam and Eve, he put them into a beautiful garden in a place called Eden. It was a park, a paradise. They could have lived there forever. But there was a lesson that they needed to learn. And it is a lesson that we need to learn too. It is not a hard one. It is easy if we really want to learn it.

Jehovah told Adam and Eve that they could

eat all the fruit and nuts that they wanted from the trees in Eden. But there was just one tree from which they were not to eat. Jehovah said to Adam: "But as for the tree of the knowledge of good and bad you must not eat from it, for in the day you eat from it you will positively die."—Genesis 2:17.

What would happen if they ate from that one tree? — They would die. Their life depended on obedience to Jehovah God. It was not enough just to say that they believed in God. They had to show it by the things they did. That was the lesson. It was not really a hard one, was it? — But it was very important.

If Adam and Eve obeyed God, they would be showing that they loved him and wanted him to be their Ruler. But if they ate from that tree, what would it show? — It would show that they really were not thankful for all the

things that God had given them. They would be saying: "Nobody can tell us what to do. We are going to do just as we please."

What would you have done if you had been there? Would you have obeyed Jehovah?

Or would you have eaten from that tree? —

At first Adam and Eve did obey God. But then a serpent or a snake spoke to Eve one day. Of course, a serpent cannot speak all by itself. It was an angel that made it seem as if the serpent was speaking. That angel had begun to think bad things. He wanted Adam and Eve to worship him. He wanted them to do the things that he said. He wanted to take God's place.

So that bad angel put wrong ideas into the mind of Eve. He said to her: 'God did not tell you the truth. You will not die if you eat from that tree. You will become wise like God.' Would you have believed what that voice said? —

Eve had no right to believe what the serpent said. Everything she had was from God. But now she began to want something that God had not given her. She ate from the tree. Then she gave some to Adam.

Adam did not believe what the serpent said. But his wanting to be with Eve was stronger than his love for God. So he ate from the tree too.—Genesis 3:1-6.

What was the result? — God had not lied. Life does depend on obedience to him. So Adam and Eve died. And they brought death to all mankind.

The Bible tells us that the angel that lied to Eve is called Satan the Devil. He is the enemy of God. And he is our enemy too.—Revelation 12:9.

He wants to make everyone disobey Jehovah. So he tries to put bad ideas into our minds. He says that nobody really loves Jehovah. He says that you and I don't love God and that we don't really want to do what God says. But is he right? Are we like that? —

The Devil says that we will quit serving Jehovah if someone makes it a little hard for us. He says that we obey Jehovah only when everything goes the way we like it. He says that everyone is like that. Is he right? —

The Great Teacher said that the Devil is a liar! He proved that there are people who really love Jehovah. He did not say: 'Nobody can tell me what to do.' Instead, he said: "The Father is greater than I am." He obeyed Jehovah. And he did not do it only when it was easy. He did it all the time, even when other people made it hard for him. He proved true to Jehovah right down till he died. That is why God brought him back to life, to live forever.—John 14:28.

That is what the Great Teacher did. But what will we do? — If we disobey Jehovah, then we are doing what the Devil wants us to do. But if we truly love our God, we will obey his commandments. We will do it every day. And we will do it because we really want to.

(Whom will we serve—Jehovah or the Devil? Read what the Bible says about this matter at Job 1:8-12; 2:1-5; 27:5; Proverbs 27:11.)

10

One Leper Gave Glory to God

DID your mother fix a good meal for you today? — It was kind of her to do that, wasn't it? — Did you thank her? — Sometimes we forget to say "Thank you" when others do kind things for us, don't we? When the Great Teacher was on earth, there were some lepers who forgot to say "Thank you."

Do you know what a leper is? — A leper is a person who has the sickness called leprosy. That sickness can even cause some of a person's flesh to fall off. When Jesus lived on earth, lepers had to live away from other people. And if a leper saw another person coming, he had to call out: 'I am a leper. Stay away!' Otherwise people might catch the leper's sickness.

Jesus was very kind to lepers. One day, on his way to Jerusalem, Jesus came near a small town. Ten lepers came out to see him.

The lepers did not come close to Jesus. They stood far off. But they had heard that Jesus had power from God to cure all kinds of sickness, even leprosy. So they called out to him, 'Jesus, Teacher, help us!'

Do you feel sorry for persons who are sick? — Jesus did. He knew how sad it was to be a leper. So he answered them, and said:

'Go and show yourselves to God's priests.'

Why did Jesus tell them to do this? — It was because of the law that Jehovah gave his people. This law said that God's priest was to look at the flesh of a leper. The priest would tell the leper when all of his sickness had left him. Then he could live with well people again. —Leviticus 13:16, 17.

But these ten lepers still had their sickness. So would they go and see the priest just as Jesus said? — Yes, they did right away. These men must have believed that Jesus would take away their sickness.

And what happened? — Well, while they were on their way to the priest, their sickness left them. Their flesh was healed. They were made well! Their belief in Jesus' power was rewarded. What joy they felt!

But, now, what should they have done to show their thanks? What would you have done? —

One of the healed men came back to Jesus. He began giving glory to Jehovah, saying good things about God. That was the right thing to do, because the power to heal him came from God. The man also fell down at the feet of the Great Teacher and thanked him. He was so grateful for what Jesus had done.

But what about the other nine men? Jesus asked: 'There were ten lepers who were made well, were there not? Where are the other nine?

Did only one turn back to give glory to God?'

Yes, it is true. Only one of the ten lepers gave glory to God, and came back to thank Jesus. And this person was a Samaritan, a man from another country. The other nine men did not thank God; at least they did not thank Jesus. —Luke 17:11-19.

Which of those men are you like? — We both want to be like the Samaritan man, don't we? — So, when someone does something kind for us, what should we remember to do? — We ought to express our thanks.

People often forget to say "Thank you." But it is good to say "Thank you." It is the right thing to do. And when you do it, Jehovah God and his Son Jesus are pleased.

If you think about it, you will remember that people have done many things for you. Do you ever remember being sick? — You may never have been as sick as those ten lepers. But you may have had a bad cold, or a pain in your stomach. Did your mother or your father take care of you? — Are you glad that they helped you to get better? —

The Samaritan man thanked Jesus for making him well, and this made Jesus happy. Do you think your mother or father will be happy if you say "Thank you" when they do things for you? — Yes, they will.

At times people do things for us every day or every week. It may be their work to do this. They may even be happy to do it. But we may forget to thank them.

Your schoolteacher may work hard to help you to learn many things. This is her work. But she will be pleased if you thank her for helping you to learn.

Sometimes people just do little things for you. Does anyone ever hold a door open for you? — Or does anyone ever pass food to you at the dinner table? — It is good to say "Thank you" for even these little things.

If we remember to say "Thank you" to people on earth, then we are more likely to remember to say "Thank you" to our Father in heaven. And how many things there are for which to thank Jehovah! He gave us our life, and all the good things that make life pleasant. So we have every reason to give glory to God by saying good things about him each day.

(As to the expressing of thanks, read also Psalm 92:1 [91:1, Dy] and Ephesians 5:20.)

11

Jesus Teaches Us to Pray

DO YOU talk to Jehovah God? — He wants you to talk to him. When you talk to God, this is called prayer.

Jesus often spoke to his Father in heaven. Sometimes he wanted to be alone when he talked to God. One time, the Bible says, "he went up into the mountain by himself to pray. Though it became late, he was there alone." —Matthew 14:23.

Where can you go to pray to Jehovah alone? — Maybe you can talk to God alone before you go to bed at night. Jesus said: "When you pray, go into your private room and, after shutting your door, pray to your Father." Do you pray to God each night before you go to sleep? — It is a good thing to do.—Matthew 6:6.

Jesus also prayed when other people were with him. When he had meetings with his disciples, Jesus would pray. You can go to Christian meetings where prayer is said. At these meetings usually an older person will pray. Listen carefully to what he says, because he is talking to God for you. Then you will be able to say "Amen" to the prayer.

Do you know what it means to say "Amen"

47

at the end of a prayer? — It means that you like the prayer. It means that you agree with it, and that you want it to be your prayer too.

Jesus also prayed at mealtimes. He thanked Jehovah for his food. Do you always pray before you eat your meals? —

It is good for us to thank Jehovah for the food before we start eating. Your father may say the prayer when you eat together. But what if you eat by yourself? Or what if you have a meal with people who do not thank Jehovah? — Then you need to say your own prayer.

Do you always have to pray out loud? — No. Jehovah can hear your prayer even if you say it in your heart. So you can say a silent prayer to Jehovah when you are with people who do not pray to God. For example, you might say a silent prayer when you eat lunch at school.

Should you bow your head when you pray? Should you get down on your knees? What do you think? —

Sometimes Jesus bent his knees when he prayed. At times he would lift his head toward heaven as he prayed. And he also spoke about praying to God while standing up.

So what does this show? Do you always have to be in the same position when you pray? — The position you are in is not the important thing. But at times it is good to bow your head. At other times you may even want to get down on your knees as Jesus did. But, remember, we can pray to God at any time during the day or night and he will hear us.

The important thing in prayer is that we really believe that Jehovah is listening. Do you believe that Jehovah hears you? —

What should we say in our prayers to Jehovah? — Tell me: When you pray, what do you talk to God about? —

Jehovah gives us so many good things, and it is right to thank him for them, isn't it? — We thank him for the food we eat. But have you ever thanked him for the blue sky, the green trees and the pretty flowers? — He made those too.

Jesus' disciples once asked him to teach them how to pray. And the Great Teacher showed them what were the most important things to

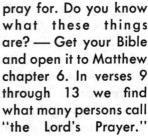

pray for. Do you know what these things are? — Get your Bible and open it to Matthew chapter 6. In verses 9 through 13 we find what many persons call "the Lord's Prayer." Let's read it together.

Here we learn that Jesus told us to pray about God's

49

name. He said to pray that God's name be sanctified or treated as holy. What is God's name? — The Bible tells us that it is Jehovah, and we should love that name.

Second, Jesus taught us to pray for God's kingdom to come. This kingdom is so important because it will bring peace to the earth and make it a paradise.

Third, the Great Teacher said to pray for God's will to be done on earth just as it is done in heaven. That means that we should do God's will.

Jesus also taught us to pray for the food we need for the day. And he said that we should tell God that we are sorry when we do things that are wrong. We should ask God to forgive us. But before he will, we must forgive others if they do wrong to us. Do you do that? —

Finally, Jesus said, we should pray that Jehovah God will protect us from the wicked one, Satan the Devil. So, all of these are good things to pray to God about.

We should believe that Jehovah hears our prayers and we should keep on thanking him, besides asking him to help us. Jehovah likes to hear us pray to him. He is happy when we mean what we say in prayer and when we ask him for the right things. And he will give us these things. Do you believe that? —

(More good counsel about prayer is found at 1 Peter 3:12, 1 John 5:14 and Romans 12:12.)

12

Tempted by the Devil

DID anyone ever ask you to do something that was wrong? — Did he dare you to do it? Or did he say it would be fun and that it would not really be wrong to do it? — When someone does this to us, he is trying to tempt us.

What should we do when we are tempted? Should we give in and do what is wrong? — That would not please Jehovah God. But do you know whom it would make happy? — Satan the Devil.

Satan is the enemy of God and he is our enemy. We cannot see him, because he is a spirit. But he can see us. One day the Devil talked with Jesus, the Great Teacher, and tried to tempt him. Let's find out what Jesus did. Then we will know the right thing to do when we are tempted.

Jesus had gone away to the mountains to pray to God. He wanted to think about the work God gave him to do.

While Jesus was there in the mountains, forty days and nights went by! All of this time Jesus did not eat anything. Jesus was now very hungry.

This is when Satan tried to tempt Jesus. The Devil said: "If you are a son of God, tell this stone to become a loaf of bread." How good some bread would taste!

But could Jesus have turned a stone into a loaf of bread? — Yes, he could. For Jesus is the Son of God. He has special powers.

Would you have made the stone a loaf of bread if the Devil asked you to do it? — Jesus was hungry. So would it have been all right to do it just once? — Jesus knew that it would be wrong to use his powers in this way. Jehovah gave him these powers to draw people to God, not to use them on himself.

So, instead, Jesus told Satan that it is written in the Bible: 'Man must live, not on bread alone, but on every word that comes forth from Jehovah's mouth.' Jesus knew that doing what pleases Jehovah is even more important than having food to eat.

But the Devil tried again. He took Jesus into Jerusalem and had him stand up on a high part of the temple. Then the Devil said to Jesus: 'If you are a son of God, throw yourself down from here. For it is written that God's angels will keep you from hurting yourself.' What did Jesus do? —

Again, Jesus did not listen to Satan. He told Satan that it was wrong to test

Jehovah by taking chances with his life.

Still Satan did not give up. He took Jesus along to a very high mountain. He showed him all the kingdoms of the world and their glory. Then Satan said to Jesus: 'All these things I will give you if you bow down and do an act of worship to me.' What would you have done? —

Jesus would not do it. He knew it would be wrong to worship the Devil no matter what he would get. So Jesus said to the Devil: 'Go away, Satan! For the Bible says, It is Jehovah your God you must worship, and you must serve only him.' —Luke 4:1-13; Matthew 4:1-10.

We are faced with temptations too. Do you know how? — Here is an example.

Your mother may make a delicious pie or cake for dinner. But she may tell you not to eat any of it until mealtime. You may be very hungry. So you may feel tempted to eat it. Will you obey your mother? — Satan wants you to disobey.

But remember Jesus. He was very hungry too. But he knew that pleasing God was more important.

As you grow a little older, it may be that some other children will ask you to swallow some pills. Or they may give you a cigarette to smoke. They may tell you that these will make you feel really good. But these things may be drugs. They can make you very sick, and can even kill you. What will you do? —

Remember Jesus. Satan tried to get Jesus to take chances with his life by telling him to jump off the temple. But Jesus would not do it. He did not listen to Satan. Neither should you listen to anyone who tries to get you to take drugs.

It is easy to do what is right when everyone else is doing it. But it can be pretty hard when others are trying to get us to do wrong. They may say that what they are doing is not so bad. But the big question is, What does God say about it? He knows best.

So no matter what others say, we will not do things God says are not right. In that way we will always make God happy, and will never serve the Devil.

(More good advice about how to resist temptation to do wrong is found at Matthew 26:41, Proverbs 22:24, 25 and Psalm 1:1, 2.)

13

Those Who Became
Jesus' Disciples

I AM thinking of the finest servant of God that ever lived on earth. Do you know who he is? — That's right. Jesus Christ.

Do you think that you and I can be like him? — Well, the Bible says that he set the example for us to follow. And he invites us to be his disciples.

What does it mean to be Jesus' disciples? — It means several things. To be Jesus' disciples, we must learn from him. But that is not all. We must really believe what he says. Do you really believe everything that Jesus says? — If we really believe, we will do what he tells us, won't we? —

Many people say that they believe in Jesus. But are all of them really his disciples? Do you think they are? —

No; most of them are not. They may go to church once in a while. But many of them have never taken time to learn what Jesus taught. If you try to talk to them about Jesus, they may say they are not interested. And they do not share in the preaching work that Jesus told his disciples to do. So they are not really his disciples.

What kind of people become disciples of Jesus? Do you know? — It would be interesting to meet some of those who were Jesus' disciples when he was a man on earth.

Some of them were fishermen. One day while Jesus was walking beside the Sea of Galilee he saw Peter and his brother Andrew. They were letting down a fishing net into the sea. Jesus called to them: "Come after me."

Going a little farther, Jesus saw two other men who were brothers. Their names were James and John. They were in a boat with their father, repairing their fishing nets. Jesus called James and John to be his disciples too.

If Jesus had called you, what would you have done? Would you have gone with Jesus right away? — These men knew who Jesus was. They knew that Jesus had been sent by God. So at once they left their fishing business and followed Jesus.—Matthew 4:18-22.

It is plain that these men were willing. They wanted to do what was right, and that is important. But they were not perfect. Consider Peter. There were times when he said the wrong thing, and it got him into trouble. But he had a good heart. He did not try to make it appear that he had done no wrong when he knew that he had done wrong. He listened and was willing to change. If we are willing like Peter, we can be disciples of Jesus too.

Jesus also spoke to a rich young ruler. Could

a man like this become a disciple of Jesus? —
He showed interest. He asked Jesus how to
gain eternal life. Jesus explained this to him. But
when the man learned that being a disciple of
Jesus had to be more important in his life than
his money, he became unhappy. Jesus invited
him: "Come be my follower." But the man did
not join him. He loved his money more than he
loved God.—Luke 18:18-25.

Jesus invited all sorts of people to be his
disciples. Even those who had lived bad lives
could change. But they must be willing to learn
and turn around and go the right way. They
must really want to please God. Is that what you
want to do? —

The only disciples that we have talked about
so far were men. Does that mean that only men
could be disciples of Jesus? — No. Women

became disciples too. The Bible even tells about a family in which four daughters were busy telling other people about God. What a happy family that must have been!—Acts 21:8, 9.

When Jesus was teaching, he took a special interest in young children. Why did he do that? — He knew that children could also become his disciples. It is true that grown-ups can do some things that children cannot do. But grown-ups are not the only ones who can learn from Jesus. And they are not the only ones who can talk about God. You can do those things too.

Do you want to be a disciple of Jesus? — I do. That is really the best thing that any of us can do.

But, remember, just saying that we are Christians does not make us disciples of the Great Teacher, does it? — If we are really his disciples, it should show in everything we do.

We will not pretend to be Christians only when we go to meetings where we talk about God, but then be bad at other times. We will live like Christians here at home.

Does being a Christian also include how you act when you play with other children? — Should it affect what a man does when he is at work? — Yes, if we are really Jesus' disciples, then we must act that way all day long, no matter where we are.

(Now read together what the Bible says about Jesus' disciples at Matthew 28:19, 20, John 8:31, 32 and Luke 6:13-15.)

14

Power over Wind and Waves

HAVE you ever been in a storm when the wind was blowing very hard? — Were you afraid? — It is good to be careful at a time like that. For you could be hurt in a bad storm.

So what should you do when the wind starts blowing hard, or when you see lightning flash from the sky? What do you think? — The wise thing to do is to go indoors. If you don't, the wind could blow down a branch of a tree on you. Or lightning could strike you. Hundreds of persons are killed every year in storms.

You and I cannot stop strong winds from blowing. And we cannot calm the big waves of the sea. In fact, there is no human alive that can do this. But did you know that there once lived on earth someone who had power over wind and waves? — It was Jesus, the Great Teacher. Would you like to hear what he did? —

Late one day after he had been teaching by the Sea of Galilee, he said to his disciples: "Let us cross to the other side of the lake." So they set out in a boat and started to sail across the lake.

Jesus was very tired. He had worked hard all day. So he went to the back of the boat and lay down on a pillow. Soon he was fast asleep.

The disciples stayed awake to keep the boat on its course. Everything was all right for a while, but then a strong wind sprang up. It blew harder and harder, and the waves kept getting bigger. The waves began splashing into the boat, and the boat started to fill up with water. The disciples were afraid they were going to sink.

But Jesus was not afraid. He was still asleep in the back of the boat. Finally, the disciples woke him up, and said: 'Teacher, Teacher, save us; we are about to die in this storm.'

At that, Jesus got up and spoke to the wind and the waves. "Hush! Be quiet!" he said. Right away the wind stopped blowing. The lake became calm.

The disciples were amazed. They had never seen anything like it before. They began saying to one another: "Who really is this, for he orders even the winds and the water, and they obey him?"—Mark 4:35-41; Luke 8:22-25.

Do you know who Jesus is? — Do you know from where he receives his great power? — The disciples should not have been afraid when Jesus was there with them, because Jesus was no ordinary man. He could do wonderful things that no other person could do. Let me tell you about something else that he once did on a stormy sea.

It was sometime later, on another day. When it became evening Jesus told his disciples to board a boat and go ahead of him to the other side of the sea. Then Jesus went up into the mountain by himself. It was a quiet place where he could pray to his Father, Jehovah God.

The disciples got into the boat, and started to sail across the sea. But soon a wind began blowing. It blew harder and harder. It was now nighttime.

The men took down the sail and began to row. But they were not getting very far, because the strong wind was blowing against them. The boat was rocking back and forth in the high waves, and water was splashing in. The men worked hard trying to reach shore, but they could not.

Jesus was still alone in the mountain. He had been there a long time. But now he could see that his disciples were in danger in the high waves. So he came down from the mountain to the edge of the sea. He did not jump in and start to swim, and he did not wade into the water. No, but Jesus started walking out over the top of the stormy sea just like we would walk on green grass!

What would happen if you tried to walk on water? Do you know? — You would sink, and you might drown. But Jesus was different. He had special powers.

Jesus had a long walk of about three or four miles to reach the boat. So it was about dawn when the disciples saw Jesus coming toward them over the water. But they couldn't believe what they saw. They were very frightened, and they cried out in their fear.

Then Jesus spoke to them: "Take courage, it is I; have no fear."

As soon as Jesus got up into the boat, the storm stopped. The disciples were again amazed. They fell down before Jesus, and said: "You are really God's Son."—Matthew 14:23-33; John 6:16-21.

Wouldn't it have been wonderful to live back then and to see Jesus do things like that? — Well, we can live at a time when Jesus will do things that are just as wonderful.

The Bible says that God has made Jesus the Ruler in the kingdom of God, and soon only his government will rule over this earth. No one who is living then will ever have to be afraid of a storm. Jesus will use his power over wind and waves for the blessing of all who obey him. Won't that be a wonderful time in which to live? —

(Other texts showing the great power of Jesus as the one whom God makes Ruler in the kingdom of God are: Matthew 28:18; Daniel 7: 13, 14; Ephesians 1:20-22.)

15

The Unforgiving Slave

HAS anyone ever done something wrong to you? — Did he hurt you or say something unkind to you? — It made you feel bad, didn't it? —

When something like that happens, should you treat the other person in the same unkind way that he treats you? — Many people would.

But the Great Teacher said that we should forgive those who do wrong to us. To show how very important it is to be forgiving, Jesus told a story. Would you like to hear it? —

Once there was a king. He was a good king. He was very kind. He would even lend money to his slaves when they needed help.

But the day came when the king wanted to get his money back. So he called his slaves who owed him money, and asked them to pay him. Well, one man owed the king sixty million pieces of money! That is a lot of money. It is more money than I have had in my whole life.

This slave had spent the king's money and had nothing with which to pay it back. So the king gave orders for the slave to be sold. The king also said to sell the slave's wife and his children and everything that the slave owned. Then with the money from the sale the king was to be paid. How do you suppose this made the slave feel? —

The slave begged the king: 'Please, do not do that to me. Give me more time, and I will pay back everything that I owe you.' If you were the king, what would you have done with the slave? —

The good king felt very sorry for his slave. So he told the slave that he did not have to pay back the money. He did not have to pay back any of the sixty million pieces of money! How happy that must have made the slave!

But what did the slave do then? He went out and found another slave who owed him just one hundred pieces of money. That is not much money at all when compared with sixty million pieces. The man grabbed his fellow slave by the neck and began to choke him. And he said to him: 'Pay back that one hundred pieces that you owe me.'

Can you imagine a person doing something like that? — The slave had been forgiven so much by the good king. And now he turned around and demanded that a fellow slave pay back one hundred pieces. This was not a kind thing to do.

Well, the slave that owed just one hundred pieces was poor. He could not pay the money back right away. So he fell down at the feet of his fellow slave and begged: 'Please give me more time, and I will pay back what I owe you.'

Should the man have given his fellow slave more time? — Would you have done it? —

Well, this man was not kind, as the king had been. Because his fellow slave could not pay him right away, he had him thrown into jail. He certainly was not forgiving.

Other slaves saw all this happen. They told the king about it. The king became very angry at the unforgiving slave. So he called him, and said: 'You bad slave, did I not forgive what you owed me? So, should you not have been forgiving to your fellow slave?'

He should have learned a lesson from the good king. But he had not. So now the king had the unforgiving slave thrown into jail until he paid back the sixty million pieces of money. And, of course, in jail he could never earn the money to pay it back. So he would stay there till he died.

As Jesus finished telling this story, he said to his followers: 'In the same way my heavenly Father will also deal with you if you do not forgive each one his brother from your hearts.' —Matthew 18:21-35.

You see, we all owe God very much. Our life

comes from God, but because we do wrong things he could take it away from us. If we tried to pay God with money, never in our whole lifetime could we earn enough to pay him what we owe him.

When compared with what we owe to God, other people owe us very little. What they owe us is like the one hundred pieces of money that the one slave owed to the other. But what we owe to God is like the sixty million pieces of money that the slave owed to the king.

God is very kind. Though we have done wrong things, he will forgive us. He will not make us pay by taking our lives away from us forever. But he forgives us only if we believe in his Son Jesus, and if we forgive other people who do wrong to us. That's something to think about, isn't it? —

So, if someone does something unkind to you, but then says that he is sorry, what will you do? Will you forgive him? — What if it happens many times? Will you still forgive him? —

If we were the person who was asking to be forgiven, we would want the other person to forgive us, wouldn't we? — We should do the same for him. We should not just say that we forgive him, but we should really forgive him from our heart. When we do that, we show that we really want to be followers of Jesus.

(To emphasize the importance of being forgiving, read also Matthew 6:14, 15, Luke 17:3, 4 and Proverbs 19:11.)

66

16

The Man Who Was Dead Four Days

ISN'T it wonderful to be alive? Do you enjoy life? — I enjoy living. When we are alive we can do so many interesting things.

But did you know that no man has lived forever? — Sooner or later all persons have died. Do you know of someone who has died? —

Once a good friend of Jesus died. This friend lived in Bethany, a small town not far from Jerusalem. His name was Lazarus, and he had two sisters, named Martha and Mary.

One day Lazarus got very sick. Jesus was far away at the time. So Martha and Mary sent word to him that their brother Lazarus was sick. Why did they do this? Because they knew that Jesus could make their brother well. Jesus was not a doctor, but he had power from God so that he could cure every kind of sickness.

But before Jesus came, Lazarus got so sick that he died. Jesus told his disciples that Lazarus was sleeping. But Jesus said that he would go to wake him up. The disciples did not understand what Jesus meant. So, then Jesus said plainly that Lazarus had died. Death is like a deep sleep, a sleep that is so deep that the person does not even dream.

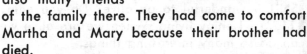

Jesus now went to visit Martha and Mary. There were also many friends of the family there. They had come to comfort Martha and Mary because their brother had died.

When Martha heard that Jesus was coming, she went out to meet him. Soon Mary also came out to see Jesus. She was very sad and was crying, and she fell at his feet. Other friends, who had followed Mary, were also crying. When Jesus saw all the people crying, he became sad and started to cry too.

The Great Teacher asked where they had laid Lazarus. At that the people led Jesus to the cave where Lazarus had been buried. Jesus then told the men there: 'Roll the stone away from the front of the cave.' Should they do it? —

Martha did not think it was right. She said: 'Lord, by now he must smell, for he has been dead four days.' And it is true that dead bodies do smell bad after a while.

But Jesus said to her: "Did I not tell you that if you would believe you would see the glory of God?" Jesus meant that Martha would see something that would bring honor to God. What was Jesus going to do?

When the stone had been removed, Jesus prayed out loud to Jehovah. Then Jesus said in a loud voice: "Lazarus, come on out!" Would he come out? Could he? —

Well, can you wake up somebody who is sleeping? — Yes, if you call in a loud voice, he will wake up. But can you wake up someone who is sleeping in death? — No. No matter how loud you call, the one who is dead will not hear. There is nothing that you or I can do to wake the dead.

But Jesus is different. He has special power from God. So, when Jesus called Lazarus, an amazing thing happened. The man who had been dead for four days came out of the cave! He had been brought back to life! He could breathe and walk and speak again! Yes, Jesus raised Lazarus after he had been dead four days! Wasn't that wonderful? — —John 11: 1-44.

But you may ask, Where was Lazarus during the four days he was dead? Did Lazarus go to heaven when he died? Was he alive up there with God and the holy angels? —

Think now: If Lazarus had been in heaven during those four days, would he not have said something about it? — And if he were in heaven, would Jesus have made him come back from that wonderful place? — The Bible does not say that Lazarus was in heaven.

Remember, Jesus said that Lazarus was

sleeping. What is it like when you are asleep? —

When you are in a very deep sleep, you do not know what is going on around you, do you? — And when you wake up you do not know how long you have been sleeping until you look at a clock.

It is like that with dead persons. They do not know anything that is happening. They do not feel anything. And they cannot do anything.

But some people are afraid of the dead. They won't go near a graveyard, because they think that the dead might harm them. Can you imagine that? Can a dead person harm someone who is alive? — No, the Bible says that the dead are not able to do anything at all.

Have you ever heard anyone say that on a certain day the dead come back as spirits to visit the living? — Some people believe that. So they set out food for the dead. Or they may have special parties on those days. But do you think that people who do those things really believe what God says about the dead? —

Do you believe what God says? — If we do, we won't be afraid of the dead, but we will be glad that we are alive. And if we are really thankful to God for life, we will show it by the way we live our lives each day. We will do the things that God approves.

(To emphasize appreciation for daily life, in contrast with the condition of the dead, read Ecclesiastes 9:5, 10, Ezekiel 18:4 and Psalm 115:17 [113:17, Dy].)

17

Two Persons Who Did Not Tell the Truth

SUPPOSE a girl promises her mother, "Yes, I will come home right after school." But then other children ask her to stay and play with them. Would it be all right to stay—just for a little while? —

Or perhaps a boy promises his father, "No, I won't throw the ball in the house anymore." Would it be all right to do it just a few more times when his father is not looking? —

The Great Teacher showed the right thing to do. He said: 'Just let your word **Yes** mean Yes, and your **No**, No; for anything else is from the wicked one.'—Matthew 5:37.

What did Jesus mean by that? — He meant that we should always keep our promises; we should always tell the truth.

There is a story that shows how important it is to tell the truth. It is about two persons who said that they were disciples of Jesus.

A short time after the death of Jesus, many people became his disciples. Some of these people had come to Jerusalem from faraway places. Here for the first time they learned about Jesus. They wanted to know more. As a result they stayed in Jerusalem longer than they had expected. Some of them ran out of money and needed help so that they could buy food.

The disciples in Jerusalem wanted to help them out. So, many of these disciples sold things that they owned and they brought the money to Jesus' apostles. Then the apostles gave the money to the ones who needed it.

A disciple named Ananias and his wife Sapphira sold a field that they owned. No one told them that they had to sell it. They decided that for themselves. But what they did was not because they loved the new disciples. Really, they wanted to make people think they were better than they really were. So they decided to make it look as if they were giving all of this money to help others. But really they were going to give only a part of it and keep the rest. What do you think of that? —

Well, Ananias came to see the apostles of Jesus first. He gave the money to them. But Ananias was not giving all the money. God knew this. So he let the apostle Peter know that Ananias was not being truthful. At that Peter said:

'Ananias, why have you let Satan cause you to do this? The field was yours. You didn't have to sell it. And even after you sold the field, it was up to you to decide what you would do with the money. But why did you pretend to give all the money when you were giving only part of it? By this you were lying, not just to us, but to God.'

It was that serious. Ananias was lying! He did not do what he said he was going to do. He and his wife only pretended to do it.

The Bible tells us what happened next. It says: 'On hearing Peter's words, Ananias fell down and died.' God struck Ananias dead! His body was carried outside and buried.

About three hours later Sapphira his wife came in. She did not know what had happened to her husband. So Peter asked her: 'Did you two sell the field for the amount of money that you gave us?'

Sapphira answered: 'Yes, we sold the field for just that amount.'

But that was a lie! They had kept some of the money for themselves. So God struck Sapphira dead too.—Acts 5:1-11.

Do you think there is something that we should learn from what happened to Ananias and Sapphira? — Yes. It teaches us that God does not like liars. He wants us always to tell the truth.

Many people say that it is not bad to tell lies. They tell lies almost every day. But do you think that is right? —

Did you know that all the sickness, pain and death that are on the earth came because of a lie? — The Devil lied to the first woman Eve about God. As a result, she broke God's law. Then she got Adam to break God's law too. Now they were sinners, and all their children would be born sinners. And because of sin they would suffer and die. How did it all start? — With a lie.

No wonder Jesus said that the Devil "is a liar and the father of the lie." He is the first one that told a lie. When anyone tells a lie, he is doing what the Devil did. We should think about this if we ever feel tempted to tell a lie.—John 8:44.

It is often when a person does something wrong that he may feel tempted to lie about it. For example, you may break something. You may not have meant to do it, but the thing broke anyway. What should you do? — Should you try to hide it and hope that no one will find out? —

We should remember Ananias and Sapphira. They tried to hide the truth. And God showed how bad that was by striking them dead.

So, no matter what we may do, we should never lie about it. The Bible says: "Speak truth." It also says: "Do not be lying to one another." Jehovah always speaks the truth, and he expects us to do the same.—Ephesians 4:25; Colossians 3:9.

(We should always tell the truth. That is the point made at Exodus 20:16; Proverbs 6:16-19; 14:5; 12:19; 16:6.)

18

Why People Do Bad Things

WOULDN'T it be wonderful if everyone were good? — Then no one would ever hurt anyone else.

But is there anyone who really is good all the time? What do you think? — The Bible tells us that Jehovah God is always good. And Jesus, the Great Teacher, always does what is right. But none of us are good all the time.

We may try to be good. But there are times when we think bad things, aren't there? — And at times we do bad things. The first man, Adam, disobeyed God on purpose. What he did was very bad. As a result, we were all born imperfect. We are all the children of Adam. That is one reason why people do bad things, even though they don't want to be bad.

But some people do bad things on purpose. They hate other people and do things to hurt them. Do you think a person like that could ever change and learn to be good? —

The Bible gives examples of bad persons who changed. I am going to tell you about one of them. And, together, let's see if we can figure out why he was bad.

The man's name was Saul. Saul was a very religious man. He belonged to a religious group called the Pharisees. They had God's Word, but they paid more attention to the teachings of some of their own leaders. Do you think that was wise? — It could lead to much trouble.

One day when Saul was in Jerusalem a disciple of Jesus named Stephen was arrested. They took him to court. Some of the judges on the court were Pharisees. Even though bad things were said about him, Stephen was not afraid. He spoke right up and gave the judges a good witness about God and about Jesus.

But those judges did not like what they heard. They became very excited. They grabbed hold of Stephen and took him outside the city. They knocked him down, and threw stones at him until they had killed him.

Saul was right there watching while Stephen was being put to death. He thought it was good to kill him. But how could he think such a bad thing? —

Well, Saul had grown up

as a Pharisee. All his life he had been taught that they were right. He looked to these men for his example. So he copied them.

Now that Stephen was dead, Saul wanted to get rid of the rest of Jesus' disciples. He began going right into their homes and dragging out both men and women. Then he would have them thrown into prison. Many of the disciples moved away from Jerusalem to get away from Saul. But they did not stop preaching about Jesus. —Acts 8:1-4.

This caused Saul to hate Jesus' disciples even more. So he went to the high priest and got permission to arrest Christians in the city of Damascus. But on the way to Damascus an amazing thing happened.

A light flashed from heaven so bright that it made Saul blind. And a voice said: "Saul, Saul, why are you persecuting me?" It was the Lord Jesus speaking from heaven! So Saul was led blind to Damascus.

Three days later Jesus appeared in a vision to one of his disciples named Ananias. Jesus told Ananias to visit Saul to take away his blindness and to talk to him. Saul was now ready to listen. When Ananias spoke to him, Saul accepted the truth about Jesus. His eyes got back their sight. His entire way of life changed. He became a faithful servant of God.—Acts 9:1-22.

Now do you see why Saul used to be so bad? — He had been taught wrong things. He was following men who were not faithful to God. And he belonged to a group of people who put the ideas of men ahead of the Word of God. But Saul changed because he did not really hate the truth.

There are many people today who are like Saul. They can change, but it is not easy. One reason is that someone is working hard to make everyone do bad. Do you know who that is? — Jesus talked about him when he spoke to Saul from heaven. He told Saul: 'I am sending you to open people's eyes, to turn them from darkness to light and from the power of Satan to God.' —Acts 26:17, 18.

Yes, it is Satan the Devil who has caused all the teaching of bad things. He wants people to be bad. So if we do what is bad, then the Devil is pleased. But we want to please Jehovah, don't we? — How can we be sure to do this? —

We will please God if we always pay attention to the Bible and do what it says. When the Bible shows that we have been doing something bad, we should stop doing it. When we learn from the Bible about things that God wants us to do, we should be eager to do them. When we do what pleases God we are doing good things, because God is good.

(For help in avoiding what is bad, read together Proverbs 3:5-7; 12:15; 2:10-14; Psalm 119:9-11 [118:9-11, Dy].)

19

Love for Our Brothers and Sisters

HOW many brothers and sisters do you have? — Not everyone has a brother or a sister in his family at home. If you have even one, you can be thankful.

God made us so that we feel especially close to certain people. We may have many friends, but brothers and sisters usually care about one another even more than friends do. When one is in trouble, the other helps out. That's the kind of brother you would want to have, isn't it? —

But not everyone is good to his brother or his sister. The Bible tells us about a person who hit his brother. Do you know his name? — He was Cain, a son of the first man.

One day Cain took some food that he had grown as a farmer. He made a gift or an offering of this food to Jehovah. His brother Abel also made an offering to Jehovah. Abel offered to God the very best sheep that he had. God was pleased with Abel and with his offering. But he was not pleased with Cain and his offering.

Why was that? — It was not because Abel

offered the most. And it was not just his offering a sheep that made the difference. The Bible tells us that God can see what is in people's hearts. He knows how we feel deep inside ourselves.

What did God see in Cain's heart? — He saw that Cain did not really love his brother. Cain could see that Jehovah was pleased with Abel and his offering. But did Cain try to change so that he would be like his brother? — No. He became angry.

Jehovah told Cain that he should change his ways. But Cain did not listen. If he had really loved God, he would have paid attention to him. But he did not love God. And he did not love his brother.

So, one day he said to Abel: "Let us go over into the field." Cain had bad in his heart, but Abel did not know it. Abel went along with Cain. While they were there in the field alone, Cain hit his brother. He hit him so hard that he killed him. Wasn't that terrible? — —Genesis 4:2-8.

The Bible tells us that there is a special lesson that we should learn from that. Do you know what it is? — 'This is the message which you have heard from the beginning: we should have love for one another; not like Cain, who came from the wicked one.' So brothers and sisters should have love for one another. They should not be like Cain.—1 John 3:11, 12.

Why would it be so bad to be like Cain? —
Because the Bible says that he 'came from the
wicked one.' Since Cain acted like the Devil,
it was just as if the Devil were his father. Think
of that!

Do you see why it is so important to love
your brothers and sisters? — If you do not love
them, whose child would you be? — You would
be a child of the Devil. You wouldn't want to
be that, would you? — So how can you prove
that you want to be a child of God? — It is by
really loving your brothers and sisters.

But what is love? — Love is a deep feeling
inside us that makes us want to do good things
for other people. We show that we
love others when we have a good
feeling toward them. We show it when
we do good things for them.
And if we really love someone,
will we hold off from doing
good to him until he first does
something for us? —

God doesn't do that. Even
before we loved God, God
loved us. We can
learn from this.
Even before others
show love for us,
we can show that
we love them.

The Bible says

that Christians have many more brothers and sisters than just those who live in the same house with them. Do you know who they are? — Jesus said: 'Whoever does the will of my Father in heaven is my brother and sister.' That means that all who do God's will are brothers and sisters. They are a special family of brothers and sisters. Did you know that? — —Matthew 12:50.

Do you love all the brothers and sisters in this big Christian family? — Jesus said that we should. He said: 'Everyone will know that you are my disciples if you love one another.' We cannot love just a few of them. We must love all of our brothers and sisters.—John 13:35.

How can we show that we really love them? — Well, if we love them, we won't stay away from them because we don't want to talk to them. We will be friendly to all of them. We will always do good to them. And if ever they are in trouble, we will come to their help, because we are truly a big family.

When we really do love all our brothers and sisters, what does it prove? — It proves that we are disciples of Jesus, the Great Teacher. And isn't that what we want to be? —

(Showing love for our brothers and sisters is also discussed at 1 John 4:8, 20, 21 and Galatians 6:10. Why not open your own Bible and read those texts?)

20

Children Raised from the Dead

ISN'T it wonderful to know that someone loves you? — It's a fine thing to have persons who really care for you. But do you know that there is someone who loves you more than anyone on earth does? — That one is Jehovah God.

How much does Jehovah love us? — Does he just think about us when we are here, and then forget us when we are gone? Or does he really remember us? — The Bible says that neither 'death nor life, nor things here nor things to come, will be able to separate us from God's love.'—Romans 8:38, 39.

So God does not forget. He remembers persons who serve him, and he remembers their little children too. Even if they should die, he will bring them back to life again.

When God's Son Jesus was on earth, he showed that Jehovah cares for little children. Jesus would take time to talk to children about God. He even used God's power to bring young ones back from the dead! Would you like to hear how Jesus did this for one family? —

There was a man named Jairus. He and his wife and their twelve-year-old daughter lived a short distance from the Sea of Galilee. The father and mother loved their daughter very much. She was their only child.

So you can imagine how sad they were when their little girl became very sick. They did everything they could to make her better, but she only got worse. Jairus could see that his daughter was going to die. And there was nothing that he or the doctors could do to help her.

But maybe Jesus could help. Jairus had heard about this wonderful man and how he could heal people. So Jairus went to look for him. He found Jesus on the shore of the Sea of Galilee teaching many people.

Jairus made his way through the crowd and fell at Jesus' feet. He said to him: 'My little daughter is very sick. Will you please come and help her? I beg you to come.'

Right away Jesus went with Jairus. The crowd that had come to see the Great Teacher also followed along. But after they had gone a distance, some men came from the house of Jairus, and told him: "Your daughter died! Why bother the teacher any longer?"

Jesus overheard the men say this. He knew how sad Jairus was to lose his only child. So he told him: 'Do not fear. Just have faith in God. Your daughter will be all right.'

So they kept on going until they came to Jairus' house. Here friends of the family were crying. They were sad because their little friend

had died. But Jesus told them: 'Stop weeping. The young child has not died, but she is sleeping.'

When Jesus said this, the people began to laugh at him. For they knew that the girl had died. But Jesus said that the girl was only sleeping in order to teach those people a lesson. He wanted them to know that by means of God's power he could bring a dead person back to life just as easily as we could wake up a person from sleep.

Jesus now had everyone leave the room except three of his apostles and the child's father and mother. Then he went in where the young child was. He took her by the hand, and said: 'Young girl, get up!' And right away she got up and began walking! The father and mother were just filled with joy.—Mark 5:21-24, 35-43; Luke 8:40-42, 49-56.

Have you ever had a friend who died? — Would you like it if that person could come back to life so that you could enjoy his company again? — Do you think this can happen? —

Since Jesus could bring that young girl back to life, he can do the same for others, can't he? — But will he really do it? — Yes, because Jesus himself said: "The hour is coming in which all those in the memorial tombs will hear his voice and come out." And that time is coming soon, under the rule of God's kingdom.—John 5:28, 29.

Just think how wonderful it will be to welcome people back to life! Some of them will be persons that we knew. And we will know who they are when they come back from the dead, just as Jairus knew his daughter when Jesus raised her. Others will be persons who died thousands of years ago. But just because they lived long ago, God will not forget them.

Isn't it wonderful to know that Jehovah God and his Son Jesus love us that much? — They want us to live, not for just a few years, but forever!

(Concerning the Bible's wonderful hope for the dead, read also Acts 24:15, 1 Corinthians 15:20-22 and Isaiah 25:8.)

21

"Your Sins Are Forgiven"

IT MAKES you feel good when you do what is right, doesn't it? — You know that your father and mother are pleased, and that Jehovah God is too. But no matter how hard we may try, sometimes we do what is wrong, don't we? — When we do what God says is wrong, this is sin.

The Great Teacher, Jesus Christ, showed that sin does something bad to all of us. He showed this when he did one of his wonderful acts or miracles.

At this time Jesus was staying in a town near the Sea of Galilee. A crowd of people came to see him there. So many people came that there was no more room for others to enter the house. No one else could even get near the door.

But more people kept coming. One group of people brought a man who was very sick. He was paralyzed. It took four men to carry him on a little bed or cot, because he could not walk.

Do you know why they wanted to bring this sick man to Jesus? — They believed that Jesus could heal him from that sickness.

But, with all those people in the house, how could they get the paralyzed man to Jesus? — The men found a way. They climbed up onto the roof. It was a flat roof. And they made a big hole in it. Then they lowered the sick man on his cot right through that hole and into the room below. What faith they had!

All the people in the house were surprised when they saw what was happening. The paralyzed man on his cot was lowered right down into the room. Was Jesus angry because of what the men had done? — Not at all! He was glad to see their faith. He said to the paralyzed man: "Your sins are forgiven."

Some of the people did not think it was right for Jesus to say that. They did not think that he could forgive sins. So, to show that he really could, Jesus said to the man: "Get up, pick up your cot, and go to your home."

When Jesus said that, the man was healed! He was not paralyzed anymore. Now he did not need other people to carry him about. He was able to get up all by himself and walk and carry his cot too.

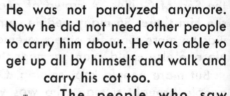

The people who saw this were amazed. Never in all their lives had they seen anything as wonderful as that. —Mark 2:1-12.

What do we learn from this miracle? — We

learn that Jesus had the power to forgive sins and to make sick persons well. But we also learn something else. We learn that people get sick because of sin.

Have you ever been sick? — Since we can all get sick, does this mean that we are all sinners? — Yes, the Bible says that we are all born in sin.

Do you know what it means to be born in sin? — It means that we are all born imperfect. We all do things wrong sometimes even though we don't want to. We got this way because the first man and woman, Adam and Eve, did not obey God. They sinned when they broke God's law. And we all got sin from Adam.

Do you know how we got our sin from him? — Let me try to explain it in a way that you can understand. Maybe you have made mud pies in a pan. What will happen to the mud pies if you make a dent in the pan? Do you know? — That same mark will show on all the mud pies you make in that pan, won't it? —

Adam was like that pan, and we are like the mud pies. He became imperfect when he broke God's law. It was as though he received a dent or a bad mark. So when he had children, what would they be like? — All his children would receive this same mark of imperfection.

Most children are not born with some big imperfection that you can see. They do not have an arm missing, or a hole in their side. But the imperfection they have is big enough so that they become sick and, in time, die.

Of course, some persons get sick more often than others. Why is that? Is it because they are born with more sin? — No. But it may be because they do not have enough food to eat. Or they may eat too much cake and candy. They may stay up too late at night and not get enough sleep. Or they may not put on the right clothing before they go out in the rain or the cold.

Will there ever be a time when we will not get sick? Will we ever get rid of sin? — Well, what did Jesus do for that paralyzed man? — He forgave his sins, and healed him. In this way Jesus showed what he is going to do for all those who try hard to do what is right.

If we show that we do not like sin, that we hate what is wrong, he will heal us. He will take away the sin that we now have. He will do this for us soon by means of the kingdom of God.

Sin will not be taken away all at once. That will be done over a period of time. Then, when our sin is finally gone, we will never get sick again. We will all have perfect health. What a blessing that will be!

(For more helpful thoughts about how sin affects everyone and what we can do about it, read Romans 3:23; 5:12; 6:12-14, 23 and 1 John 2:1.)

22

The Man Who Forgot God

THERE was a man who came to see Jesus one day. He knew that Jesus was very wise. He said to Jesus: 'Teacher, tell my brother to give me some of the things he has.' The man thought he had a right to some of those things.

If you were Jesus, what would you have said? — Jesus saw that the man had a problem. But the problem was not that he needed what his brother had. The man's problem was that he did not know what was truly important in life.

So Jesus told him a story. It was about a man who forgot God. Would you like to hear it? —

A certain man was very rich. He owned lands and barns. The crops that he planted grew very well. He did not have room in his barns to store all the crops. What was he going to do?

The rich man said to himself: 'I will tear down my barns and build bigger ones. Then I will store my crops and all my good things in these new barns.'

The rich man thought that this was the wise thing to do. He thought that he was very smart to store up many things. He said to himself: 'I have many good things stored up. They will last me for many years. So now I can take it easy. I will eat, drink and enjoy myself.'

But there was something wrong with the rich man's thinking. What was it? — He was thinking only about himself and his own pleasure. But he forgot God.

So God spoke to the rich man. He told him: 'You foolish man. You are going to die tonight. Then who will have the things that you stored up?'

Could that rich man use those things after he died? — No; someone else would get them. Jesus said: "So it goes with the man that lays up treasure for himself but is not rich toward God."—Luke 12:13-21.

You do not want to be like that rich man, do you? — His main purpose in life was the getting of material things. That was his mistake. He always wanted more.

Many people are like that rich man. They always want more. But this can lead to big problems.

For example, you have toys, don't you? — What are some of the toys that you have? Tell me. —

What if one of your friends has a model truck, or a doll or some other toy that you don't have? Would it be right for you to try to get it away from him? —

There may be times when a toy seems very important. But what happens to it after a while? — It gets old. It may fall apart, and then we do not even want it anymore. Really, you have something that is much more precious than toys. Do you know what that is? — It is your life. And your life depends on doing what pleases God, doesn't it? — So don't be like that foolish rich man.

It is not only children who do things like that rich man. A lot of grown-ups do too. Some of them always want more than they have. They may have food for the day, clothing to wear and a place to live. But they want more. They want lots of clothes. And they want bigger houses. These things cost money. So they work hard to get lots of money. And the more money they get, the more they want.

Some grown-ups become so busy trying to get money that they have no time to be with their family. And they have no time for God. Can their money keep them alive? — No; only God can do that. Can they use their money after they die? — No; because the dead are not able to do anything at all.

Does that mean that it is wrong to have money? — No. We can buy food with it. We buy clothing with it. The Bible says that having money is a protection. But if we "love" money, then we are going to have trouble. We will be like that foolish rich man who stored up treasures for himself and was not rich toward God.—Ecclesiastes 7:12.

The Great Teacher said that the rich man was foolish because he was not "rich toward God." What does it mean to be "rich toward God"? — It means to put God first in our lives. Some people say that they believe in God. They may even read from the Bible once in a while. And they think that is enough. But are they really "rich" toward God? —

A person who is rich has more than a little bit. He has much. If he is "rich toward God," his life is filled with lots of thoughts about God. He enjoys talking about God often. He is always doing the things that God tells him to do. And he spends his time with people who love God.

Is that the kind of people we are? Are we "rich toward God"? — If we really learn from the Great Teacher, we will be.

(Here are some more texts that show the proper view to have toward material things: 1 Timothy 6:6-10; Proverbs 23:4; 28:20; Hebrews 13:5.)

23

The Blessing of Work

WHICH would you rather do, work or play? — It's true that we all enjoy playing. But would it really be good if we played all the time? — Have you ever thought what would happen if no one ever worked? —

Think about the food you eat. Do you know where it comes from? — Most of it grows on plants and trees. But if no one cared for them and picked the fruits and vegetables, what would you eat? Isn't it good that people work so that you have food to eat? —

Look around the home in which you live. Do you have a bed to sleep on? — Are there chairs on which to sit and also a table? — Aren't you glad someone worked to make these things? —

How did the Great Teacher feel about work? Let's see.

Even as a boy he worked in a carpenter shop. He made things out of wood. Joseph was a carpenter, and he raised Jesus as his own son. That's why the Bible calls Jesus "the carpenter's son." In those days a young boy would learn to do the same jobs his father did.—Matthew 13:55.

It may have been hard for Jesus at first. But with practice, he learned to do the work well.

Jesus became a carpenter too.—Mark 6:3.

Do you think this work brought Jesus pleasure? — Would you be happy if you could make fine tables and chairs and other things for people to use? — The Bible says it's good for one to "rejoice in his works." Work gives a kind of pleasure that you cannot get from play. It's not wrong to play, but it's not good to play all the time.—Ecclesiastes 3:22.

Jesus did not work as a carpenter all his life. Jehovah God had special work for him to do on earth. Do you know what that work was? — Jesus said: "I must declare the good news of the kingdom of God, because for this I was sent forth." Yes, God had a preaching work for Jesus to do.—Luke 4:43.

How did Jesus feel about doing this work? Did he want to do it? —

Jesus said: "My food is for me to do the will of him that sent me and to finish his work." How much do you like to eat your favorite food? — This gives you an idea of how much Jesus liked the work that God gave him.—John 4:34.

God made us so that we are happy when we learn to work. He says that it is his gift to man that he should "rejoice in his hard work." So, if you learn to work when you are young, your whole life will be more enjoyable.—Ecclesiastes 5:19.

That does not mean that a young child can do the work of a big man, but we can all do some work. Your father works day after day so that we will have food to eat and a home in which to live. Do you know what kind of work your father does? — He doesn't work just for himself. He works for the good of the whole family. And your mother works to prepare our meals. She keeps our home and our clothing clean.

What work is there that you can do that will be a blessing to the whole family? — You can help to set the table, wipe the dishes, clean your room and pick up your toys. Perhaps you already do some of those things. Is that work really a blessing? —

Let's see how work like that is a blessing. Toys are to be put away after you play. Why would you say that is important? — It helps to make the house neat. It is also important because it can prevent accidents. If you don't pick up your toys, your mother may come along someday with her arms full and step on one of them. She may trip and fall and hurt her head. She may even have to go to the hospital. Wouldn't that be terrible? — So, when you put away your toys after you play, that is a blessing to all of us.

There is other work that children have too. I am thinking of schoolwork. At school you learn how to read. Some children find reading to be fun, but some say it is hard. Even if it seems hard at first, you will be glad if you learn to read well. When you know how to read, there are so many interesting things that you can learn. You will even be able to read God's own book, the Bible, for yourself. So, when you do your schoolwork well, it is really a blessing, isn't it? —

There are some people who try to avoid work. Maybe you know someone who does that. But since God made us to work, we need to learn how to enjoy work.

Here are some things that can help. When you have work to do, ask yourself: Now, why does this need to be done? When you know why something is important, it is easier to do it. And whether the work is big or little, do a good job of it. If you do that, you can rejoice in the work of your hands. Then you will know for yourself that work really is a blessing.

(The Bible can help a person to become a good worker. Read what it says at Colossians 3:23; Proverbs 10:4; 22:29; Ecclesiastes 3:12, 13, 22.)

24

Help from God's Angels

SOME people say that they believe only what they can see. But that is foolish. There are lots of real things that we have never seen with our eyes. Can you name one? —

What about the air? We breathe it. Can we feel it? — Hold up your hand. Now I'll blow on it. Did you feel it? — Yes, but we can't see the air, can we? —

Are there also people that we can't see? — Yes. God is one. I have never seen him, but I have seen the things that he has made. You have seen those things too, haven't you? — So we know that God is real.

And the Bible says that God made lots of persons to live with him in heaven. God can see them, and they can see God. But he made them so that we could not see them. He also made them very strong, much stronger than men. They are called angels.

The Great Teacher knew about angels. When he was in heaven he was an angel. And he lived with the other angels. He knew millions of them. And those angels are interested in us if we serve Jehovah.

There was a man named Daniel who served Jehovah. Daniel lived in Babylon. Many people there did not love Jehovah. They even had Daniel thrown into a lions' den because he would not stop praying to Jehovah. There Daniel was with all those hungry lions. What would happen? 'God sent his angel and shut the mouths of the lions.' Daniel was not hurt at all! Angels can do wonderful things.—Daniel 6:18-22.

Another time Peter was in jail. Peter was an apostle of the Great Teacher. Some people did not like it when he told them that Jesus was the Son of God. So they put Peter in jail. Soldiers were guarding Peter to make sure that he didn't get away. Was there anyone who could help Peter? —

Peter was sleeping between two guards, and there were chains on his hands. But the Bible says: 'Look! Jehovah's angel came, and a light began to shine in the prison cell. Touching Peter on his side, the angel woke Peter up, saying, "Get up! Quick!" '

At that, Peter's chains fell off his hands! And the angel said to him: 'Dress yourself, put on your sandals and follow me.' The guards couldn't stop them because the angel helped Peter. Now they came to an iron gate, and a

strange thing happened. The gate opened by itself! Peter and the angel went out. That angel had set Peter free.—Acts 12:4-11.

Will the angels help us too? — Yes, they will. Does that mean that they will never let us get hurt at all? — If you were to run out in the street in front of a car, would an angel protect you? — No. Angels do not stop us from getting hurt if we do foolish things. If you jumped off a tall building, would the angels catch you? — The Devil tried to get Jesus to do that once. But Jesus wouldn't do it. We can learn from that. —Luke 4:9-13.

God has given the angels special work to do. The Bible talks about an angel who tells people everywhere to worship God.—Revelation 14: 6, 7.

How do angels do that? Do they shout from heaven so that everyone can hear them? — No; but true Christians on earth talk to others about God, and the angels guide them in their work. The angels make sure that those who really want to know about God have a chance to hear. We can share in that work, and the angels will help us.

But what if people who do not love God make trouble for us? What if they were to put us in jail, as they did to Peter? Would the angels set us free? — They could. But that is not what they always do.

One time when the apostle Paul was a

prisoner, the angels did not set him free right away. There were people in prison who needed to hear about God and Christ. There were rulers who needed to hear too. Paul would be taken before them, and he could preach to them. But the angels always knew where Paul was, and they helped him. They will help us too, if we really serve God.—Acts 27:23-25.

There is another big work that the angels will do too, and they are going to do it soon. God's time to destroy all wicked people is very near. All who do not worship the true God will be destroyed. Those who say they do not believe in angels because they cannot see them will find out how wrong they are. But it will be too late. None of the wicked will get away. The angels will find them all.—2 Thessalonians 1:6-8.

What will that mean to us? — If we are on the same side as the angels, they will be like brothers to us. There will be nothing to fear. They will help us.

But are we on that side? — We are if we serve Jehovah. And, if we serve Jehovah, we will be telling other people to serve him too.

(To learn more about how angels influence the lives of men, read Psalm 34:7 [33:8, Dy], Matthew 18:10 and Acts 8:26-31.)

25

Those Who Chose the Best Places

SOME persons always want the best things for themselves. They will take these things before anyone else can get them. Have you noticed this? — I have.

For example, at a meal I have seen a big dish being passed. It was filled with delicious pieces of cake. As the dish came around, each person carefully looked over the pieces to make sure that he took the biggest one. Do you think it is right to do that? —

There is something else that I have seen happen. A father and mother have taken their children with them to visit a friend. When they came into the friend's house, the children hurried to get the most comfortable chairs. Is this right? —

When the Great Teacher was on earth something like that happened. He was invited to a big meal at the house of an important Pharisee. There were many guests invited. As the guests came in for the meal, Jesus noticed that they would choose the best places near the head of the table. They wanted places of honor. Would you like to hear what Jesus said to them? —

He told them a story. It had good advice for those guests, and it has some good advice for us today.

Jesus said: 'Someone may invite you to a big wedding feast. When you go, do not pick the most honored place to sit. For someone more important than you may also have been invited. Then the one putting on the feast may come over to you and say, "Let this man have your place." You will then feel ashamed as all the others watch you go to the lowest place.'

Jesus wanted to show the guests the right thing to do. So he went on to say to them:

'When you are invited to a wedding feast go and sit down at the lowest place. Then the one who has invited you may come and say, "Friend, we have a better place than this for you!" You will then have honor in front of all the others as you move up to the better place.'—Luke 14:1-11.

Did you get the point of Jesus' story?— Let's take an example, and see if you did. Let's say that we were going to have dinner at someone's house. Would you pick the best place when you

were ready to sit down? Or would you leave the best place for someone else? — What do you think Jesus would want you to do? —

Take another example. Imagine that you are getting on a crowded bus. Should you hurry to get a seat, and let an old person stand? — Would Jesus want you to do that? —

Someone may say that it does not make any difference to Jesus what we do. But do you believe that? — When Jesus was at that big meal at the home of the Pharisee, he watched the people as they chose their seats. And don't you think that he is just as interested in what we do today? — Now that Jesus is in heaven he certainly is in a better position to watch us.

When each one tries to get the best place, it can cause trouble. Sometimes this happens when children go for a car ride together. As soon as the car door is opened, they rush to get the best seats, the ones near the window. And right away there is an argument. They become angry with one another because they each want the best place.

This can also happen when children go out to play a game of ball. Before they even get started playing they may have an argument over who is going to be first. Isn't it too bad that these things happen? —

Always wanting to be first can cause a lot of trouble. It even caused trouble among Jesus' apostles. Did you know that? —

Jesus had to give them all some good advice. Jesus told them that the rulers of the nations love to be big and important. They want everyone to obey them. But Jesus told his followers that they should not be that way. Rather, Jesus said: "Whoever wants to be first among you must be the slave of all." Think of that!—Mark 10:35-45.

Do you know what a slave does? — He serves other persons, rather than let others serve him. He takes the lowest place, not the first place. He acts as the least important one, not the most important. And remember that Jesus said that the one who wants to be first should act like a slave toward others.

Now, what do you think that means for us? — Would a slave argue with his master over who is going to get the best seat? — Or would he argue about who is going to eat first? — Jesus showed that a slave always puts his master before himself. Isn't that the way we should do too? — —Luke 17:7-10.

Yes, it is the Christian way to put others ahead of ourselves. This is what the Great Teacher did. And if we follow his example we will be pleasing to God.

(More texts encouraging us to put others ahead of ourselves are found at Romans 12:3 and Philippians 2:3, 4.)

26

Children Who Praise God

HAVE you ever stopped to think why you have a mouth? How do you use it? —

It is certainly true that we need the mouth for eating. But the mouth isn't only for eating. Most of us eat just a few times a day. But isn't it true that you use your mouth much more for talking? — Your lips, your tongue, the teeth, the roof of your mouth, and much more, all play a part every time you talk.

Just think what it would be like if you could not talk. How sad it would be if you could never tell anyone else what you were thinking! Aren't you glad that Jehovah gave us a mouth? — And since he gave us our mouth, don't you agree that it ought to be used in a way that will honor him? —

That is the way King David felt. He was a servant of God. And he said: "The praise of Jehovah my mouth will speak." Do you agree that this is a good thing to do with our mouths? — Then, let's repeat together what he said: "The praise of Jehovah my mouth will speak."—Psalm 145:21.

There was a young Israelite girl who used her mouth in that way. When she was living, the nation of Syria and the nation of Israel were enemies. One day the Syrians fought against Israel and took that young girl captive. She was sent to the house of the army chief, who was called Naaman. There she came to be the servant of Naaman's wife.

Now, Naaman had the sickness called leprosy. None of the doctors had been able to help him. But the young girl from Israel had great faith in Jehovah. She knew that he could do wonderful things. And she believed that one of God's special servants, a prophet, could help Naaman. Of course, Naaman and his wife did not believe in Jehovah. They had another religion. Should the young girl tell them what she knew?  Maybe they wouldn't even want to hear it. What would you have done? —

She knew that she should talk. It would be the kind thing to do. And it would show her love for God. So she said: 'If only Naaman could go to Jehovah's prophet in Israel. In that case he could be healed from his leprosy.'

Naaman wanted very much to be healed. So he listened to the girl. He went to Jehovah's prophet. When he did what the prophet told him to do, he was healed. This caused Naaman to become a worshiper of the true God. How glad he must have been that the young girl from Israel had not been afraid to praise Jehovah! —2 Kings 5:1-15.

Would you like to help someone to learn about Jehovah as that young girl did? — Who is there that you could help? —

Of course, at first they might not think that they need help. But you could talk to them about the good things that Jehovah does. And they might listen. Wouldn't it be wonderful if they came to love Jehovah as you do? — Things like that happen when you use your mouth to praise Jehovah.

The Bible also tells about a young man named Timothy. His father was not a believer in Jehovah. But his mother was, and so was his grandmother. Timothy listened to them. And from the time he was very small he knew the Bible. We need to know the Bible in order to praise Jehovah. It is the Bible that tells us about him.

As Timothy grew up, he became a fine young man. One day Paul, an apostle of Jesus Christ, visited the town where Timothy lived. He noticed how much Timothy wanted to serve Jehovah. So he invited this young man to come with him to serve God in an even bigger way. They traveled together to other places. Everywhere they told people about the kingdom of God and about Jesus.—Acts 16:1-5.

Timothy learned much about how to praise God from the apostle Paul. He saw Paul give talks to large groups of people. He saw how Paul went to people's homes to teach them too. But Timothy did not just watch. He shared in the work. As Paul said, 'Timothy is doing the work of Jehovah, even as I am.'—1 Corinthians 16:10.

Not everyone liked it when Timothy talked about God. But he did not quit. He did not say he wanted to go home. He was glad that he could use his mouth to speak the praise of Jehovah.

Now, some people may say that this is something that is only for older folks to do. But do you believe that? — The Great Teacher knew that wasn't so. One day when some people tried to get young boys to quit praising God, Jesus said: 'Did you never read in the Scriptures, "Out of the mouths of little children will come forth praise"?'—Matthew 21:16.

All of us can praise Jehovah if we really want to. It isn't hard. God gave us a mouth with which to speak. We don't have to know everything about the Bible before we start. We can just tell others what we have already learned. Would you like to do that? —

(Other scriptures that encourage young folks to serve God are Psalm 148:12, 13; Ecclesiastes 12:1; 1 Timothy 4:12.)

27

Hated for Doing Good

DO YOU love what is good? — Both of us would say that we do, wouldn't we? But do we really love it so much that we would do what is good even if others hated us for it? — It takes courage to do that, doesn't it? —

Do you think the Great Teacher had that kind of courage? Did he do good even when others hated him for it? —

Often people liked Jesus for the good things he did. Once all the people of a city gathered right at the door of the house where he was staying. They came because Jesus had been making sick people well.—Mark 1:33.

But sometimes what Jesus taught showed that the people did not believe the truth. Did everyone like to hear him then? — Were they willing to change their beliefs? — Not everyone was. In fact, some of them showed real hate for Jesus because he spoke the truth.

This happened one day in Jesus' own city of Nazareth. Jesus went into the synagogue. The synagogue is where the Jewish people met.

Jesus stood up and gave a fine talk from the Scriptures. The people at first liked it. They were amazed at the beautiful words that came out of his mouth. They could hardly believe that this was the young man who had grown up in their own city.

But then Jesus said something else. He told about times when God showed special favor to people who were not Jews like them. When Jesus said this, those in the synagogue became angry. Do you know why? —

They thought they were the only ones to have God's special favor. They thought that they were better than other people. So they hated Jesus for what he said. And do you know what they tried to do to him? —

The Bible says: 'They grabbed Jesus and rushed him outside the city. They led him to the edge of the mountain and were going to throw him over the side and kill him! But Jesus got away from them.'—Luke 4:16-30.

If that had happened to you, would you ever have gone back to talk to those people about God again? — That would take courage, wouldn't it? — Well, about a year later Jesus did go back to Nazareth. And the Bible says: "He began to teach them in their synagogue." Jesus did not stop speaking the truth because of fear of men who had no love for God. —Matthew 13:54.

On another day Jesus was in a place where there was a man whose hand was all withered up or crippled. Jesus had power from God to heal that man. But some men who were there were trying to make trouble for Jesus. What

would the Great Teacher do? —

First he showed what was the right thing to do. He asked: 'If you had a sheep that fell into a big hole on the sabbath, would you lift it out?'

Yes, they would do that for a sheep, even on the sabbath, the day when they were supposed to rest. So Jesus said: 'It is even better to help a man on the sabbath, because a man is worth more than a sheep!' How clear it was that Jesus should help this man by healing him!

So Jesus told the man to stretch out his hand. Right away it was made well like the other one! How happy that man was!

But what about those other men? Were they glad? — No. They hated Jesus even more. They went out and made plans to kill him!—Matthew 12:9-14.

People are like that today. Some like what is right. Others do not. No matter what we do, we can never please them all. So we have to decide whom we really want to please.

Whom do you want as your friends? Do you want good people for friends? — Do you want Jehovah God to be your friend? — Then you must always do what is right.

But if you do good, will the Devil like

you? — And, really, do you want the Devil to like you? —

There are people whom the Devil likes. The Bible calls them "the world." "The world" is made up of all the people who are not followers of the Great Teacher. The Great Teacher said: "If you were part of the world, the world would be fond of what is its own. Now because you are no part of the world, but I have chosen you out of the world, on this account the world hates you."—John 15:18, 19.

Some people of the world say they believe in Jesus, but they do not teach others the truth about God, as Jesus did. If you show them from the Bible that they are not teaching the truth, will they like that? — No, most of them won't. But you may find someone like that man with the withered hand. He was grateful that Jesus did not hide the truth.

There are many people who do hide the truth. They are afraid of what other people think. They are so worried about what other people may say that they hold back all their lives from doing what they know is right. What a shame! They miss out on so much happiness in life. And they miss out on the approval of God too. We don't want to be like that, do we? —

(Read together these scriptures to show that we should never let fear of what other people might think hold us back from doing what is right: Proverbs 29:25; 1 Samuel 15:24 [1 Kings 15:24, Dy]; Matthew 26:69-75; John 12:42, 43.)

28

A Loving Shepherd

DO YOU ever feel lonely? — Do you ever wonder if anybody loves you anymore? —

Or have you ever been lost? — How did you feel? — It can make you scared, can't it? —

The Great Teacher once told a story about one that was lost. But it was not a child who was lost. It was a sheep.

You know what a sheep is, don't you? — It's a small animal from which man gets wool. In some ways you are like a sheep. How is that?

Well, sheep are not big or very strong. And they get scared when they are lost. They need love and kindness. And they need someone to take care of them and to protect them, just as you do. The man who takes care of sheep is called a shepherd.

In his story Jesus told about a shepherd who had a hundred sheep. But then one of the sheep got lost. It may have been busy eating grass when the others left. Or it may just have wanted to see what was on the other side of the hill. But before that sheep knew it, it was away from the others. Can you imagine how that little one felt when it looked around and saw that it was all alone? —

What would the shepherd do when he found that one sheep was missing? Would he say that it was all the sheep's fault anyway so he wasn't going to worry about it? Or would he leave the ninety-nine sheep in a safe place and go looking for just the one? Would one sheep be worth that much trouble? — If you were that lost sheep, would you want the shepherd to look for you? —

The shepherd loved all of his sheep very much, even the one that was lost. So he went in search of the missing one.

Think how glad that lost sheep was when it saw its shepherd coming. And Jesus said that the shepherd rejoiced that he had found his sheep. He rejoiced over it more than over the ninety-nine sheep that had not got lost.

Now, who is there that is like that shepherd in Jesus' story? Who cares for us as much as that shepherd did for his sheep? — Jesus said that his Father in heaven does. And his Father is Jehovah God.

Jehovah is the Great Shepherd of his people. He loves all those who serve him, even young ones like you. He does not want any of us to be hurt or destroyed. Isn't it wonderful to know that God cares for us that much? — —Matthew 18:12-14.

Do you really believe in Jehovah God? — Is he a real Person to you? —

It is true that we cannot see Jehovah. This is

because he is a Spirit. He has a body that is invisible to our eyes. But he is a real Person, and he can see us. He knows when we need help. And we can talk to him in prayer, just as you talk to your father and mother. Jehovah wants us to do this.

So, if you ever feel sad or all alone, what should you do? — Talk to Jehovah. Draw close to him. And he will comfort and help you. Remember that Jehovah loves you, even when you feel as if you are all alone.

Now, let's get our Bibles. We are going to read together something that should warm our hearts. Turn to the twenty-third Psalm, and we'll start with the first verse.*

There it says: "Jehovah is my Shepherd. I shall lack nothing. In grassy pastures he makes me lie down; by well-watered resting places he conducts me. My soul he refreshes. He leads me in the tracks of righteousness for his name's sake. Even though I walk in the valley of deep shadow, I fear nothing bad, for you

* Psalm 22, Douay Version.

117

are with me; your rod and your staff are the things that comfort me."

That's the way people feel if their God is Jehovah. Is that the way you feel? —

As a loving shepherd takes care of his flock, so Jehovah takes good care of his people. They feel refreshed because of the good things that he does for them. He shows them the right way to go, and they gladly follow. Even when there is trouble all around them, they are not afraid. A shepherd uses his rod or his staff to protect the sheep from animals that might harm them. And God's people know that he will protect them. They feel safe because God is with them.

Jehovah really loves his sheep, and he tenderly cares for them. The Bible says: 'Like a shepherd he will lead his own sheep. With his arms he will collect the little ones together. The young ones he will help along with care.'—Isaiah 40:11.

Doesn't it make you feel good to know that Jehovah is like that? — Do you want to be one of his sheep? —

Sheep listen to the voice of their shepherd. They stay close to him. Do you listen to Jehovah? — Do you stay close to him? — Then you never need to be afraid. Jehovah will be with you.

(Jehovah lovingly cares for those who serve him. Read together what the Bible says about this at Psalms 37:25 [36:25, Dy]; 55:22 [54:23, Dy]; Isaiah 41:10; Luke 12:29-31.)

29

Make Friends with Those Who Love God

TELL me who some of your friends are. What are their names? —

It is good to have friends. They are people with whom you like to spend time. You like to talk with them and do things together.

It is also important to have the right kind of friends. How can we tell if they are the right kind or not? —

Well, who would you say is the most important person in our lives? — It is Jehovah God, isn't it? Our life, our breath and all good things come from him. We never want to do anything that would spoil our friendship with God, do we? — But did you know that our choice of friends could spoil that friendship? — That's right. So we need to choose friends carefully.

The Great Teacher showed us how to do that. He had the right kind of friends. He said: "You are my friends if you do what I am commanding you." Why was that? — Because everything that Jesus told people came from God. So Jesus was saying that his friends were people who did what God said they should do.—John 15:14.

This does not mean that Jesus was not kind to

people who were not busy in God's service. He was. He would even go to their homes and eat with them. Some people who heard about this said that Jesus was 'a friend of sinners.' But was this really true? — —Matthew 11:19.

No, it was not. Jesus didn't go to their homes because he liked the way they lived. He visited them so that he could talk to them about God. He tried to help them to change from their bad ways and to serve God.

This happened one day in the city of Jericho. Jesus was just passing through on his way toward Jerusalem. There was a crowd of people there, and in the crowd was a man named Zac·chae'us. He wanted to get a look at Jesus. But Zacchaeus was very small and he could not see because of the crowd. So he ran ahead along the road and climbed a tree in order to get a good look when Jesus went by.

When Jesus came to that tree he looked up and said: 'Hurry and get down. Today I will come to your house.' But Zacchaeus was a rich man who had done bad things. Why did Jesus want to go to the house of such a man? —

It was not because Jesus liked the way that man lived. He went there to talk to Zacchaeus about God. He saw how hard that man had tried to see him. So he knew that Zacchaeus would probably listen. This would be a good time to talk to him about the way that God says we should live.

What was the result? Zacchaeus changed from his bad ways. He gave back money he had no right to take, and he became a follower of Jesus. It was only then that Jesus and Zacchaeus became friends.—Luke 19:1-10.

So, if we learn from the Great Teacher, will we ever visit with people who are not our friends? — Yes. But we won't go to their house because we like the way they live. And we won't do wrong things with them. We will visit them so that we can talk to them about God.

But our close friends are the ones with whom we specially like to spend our time. We have seen that for them to be the right kind of friends, they must be the kind that God would like. But how can we tell if they are? —

Well, one good way is to ask them: Do you love Jehovah? Some of them may not even know who Jehovah is. But if they want to learn about him, we can help them. And when the time comes that they love Jehovah as we do, then we can become close friends.

There is another way to find out if a person

would make a good friend. Watch the things that he does. Does he do unkind things to other people and then laugh about it? That's not right, is it? — Is he always getting into trouble? We wouldn't want to get into trouble with him, would we? — Or does he do bad things on purpose and then think he is smart because he didn't get caught? Even if he didn't get caught, God saw what he did, didn't he? — Do you think that persons who do such things would be good friends? —

Why not get your Bible, and let's see what it says about how our companions affect our lives? The scripture is at First Corinthians chapter 15, verse 33. Do you have it? —

It reads: "Do not be misled. Bad associations spoil useful habits." That means that if we go with bad people we are going to become bad. And it is also true that good companions help us to form good habits.

Let's never forget that the most important person in our life is Jehovah. We don't want to spoil our friendship with him, do we? — So we must be careful to make friends only with those who love God.

(The importance of the right kind of companions is also made clear at 1 John 2:15, 2 Chronicles 19:2 [2 Paralipomenon 19:2, Dy] Psalm 119:115 [118:115, Dy] and 2 Timothy 2:22. Read those scriptures together.)

30

Two Men Who Celebrated Birthdays

DO YOU like to have parties? — If they are good parties, they can be lots of fun.

But not all parties are good. Some parties are so noisy that the people next door get angry. And there are some parties that even God does not approve. Did you know that? — Would you want to be at a party if you knew that God did not approve of it? —

The Bible tells about parties. The Great Teacher went to a party once, and so did his apostles. It was a party that was held when someone got married. Have you ever been to that kind of party? —

The Bible also tells about two birthday parties. Was one of them to celebrate the birthday of the Great Teacher? — No. Both of these birthday parties were for men who did not serve Jehovah.

One of the birthday parties was for King Herod Antipas. He was the ruler of the district of Galilee when Jesus lived there.

King Herod did many bad things. He took the wife of his brother for himself. Her name was Herodias. God's servant John the Baptist told

Herod that it was wrong for him to do that. Herod did not like that. So he had John locked up in prison.—Luke 3:19, 20.

While John was in prison, the day came for remembering Herod's birth. Herod gave a big party. He invited many important people. They all ate and drank and enjoyed themselves.

Then the daughter of Herodias came in and danced for them. Everyone was so pleased with her dancing that King Herod wanted to give her a big gift. He called her and said: 'Whatever you ask me for, I will give it to you, up to half my kingdom.'

What would she ask for? Would it be money? pretty clothes? a palace of her own? The girl did not know what to say. So she went to her mother Herodias and said: "What should I ask for?"

Now, Herodias hated John the Baptist very much. So she told her daughter to ask for his head. The girl went back to the king and said: 'I want you to give me right away on a plate the head of John the Baptist.'

King Herod did not want to kill John, because he knew that John was a good man. But Herod had made a promise, and he was afraid of what others at the party would think if he changed his mind. So he sent a man out to the prison to chop off the head of John. Soon the man came back. He had John's head on a plate, and he gave it to the girl. Then the girl ran and gave it to her mother. Wasn't that terrible?—Mark 6:17-29.

But what about the other birthday party that the Bible tells about? Was it better? —

This party was for a king of Egypt. At his party he had someone's head chopped off too. And then he hung him up for the birds to eat. —Genesis 40:20-22.

Do you think that God approved of those parties? — Would you have wanted to be at them? —

Now, we know that everything that is in the Bible is there for a reason. It tells us about good people so that we can copy them. And it tells us about bad people so that we will not do what they did. The Bible tells about just two birthday parties, and both were bad. So, what would you say that God is telling us about birthday parties? Does God want us to celebrate birthdays? —

It is true that at such parties today people do not chop off someone's head. But the whole idea of celebrating birthdays started with people who did things like that. They were pagans. They were people who did

not serve Jehovah. Do we want to be like them? —

What about the Great Teacher? Did he celebrate his birthday? — No. There is no place in the Bible that says anything about a birthday party for Jesus.

Even after Jesus died, his true followers did not celebrate his birthday. They did not want to be like the pagans. But later there were men who wanted to celebrate Jesus' birthday. They could not use the real date of Jesus' birth, because the Bible does not say when it was. So they chose a date when the pagans had a holiday. It was December 25. Even today, that is when people celebrate Christmas. Do you think God approves of that? —

Most people know that Christmas is not the birthday of Jesus. But many celebrate it anyway. They do not really care what God thinks. But we want to please Jehovah, don't we? —

So, when we have parties we want to make sure that they are good ones. We can have them anytime of the year. We don't have to wait for a special day. We can eat some special food and have fun playing games. Would you like to do that? — But before we make our plans, let's be sure that it is the kind of party that God would approve.

(The importance of always doing what God approves is also shown at John 8:29, Romans 12:2, Proverbs 12:2 and 1 John 3:22.)

31

Water Sweeps Away a World

DO YOU like to play games? — I do. They can be a lot of fun, can't they? — But did you know that there is danger in becoming too busy having fun? — Yes, there is. We might fail to take time to listen to God. Did you know that? —

The Great Teacher knew that this had happened to a whole world of people once before. He said: 'Those people were eating. They were drinking. They were getting married.' It is not wrong to eat and to drink or to get married. But they were so busy doing those things that they did not take time to listen to God. That was bad.

What happened to those people? — Jesus said: "They took no note until the flood came and swept them all away." Jesus was talking about the people who died in the days of Noah. At that time the waters of a flood covered the whole earth.—Matthew 24:37-39.

Jesus said that what happened to those people is a lesson for us today. So it is important that we know all about the flood of Noah's day.

First of all, why did Jehovah God bring the flood? — It was because the people were doing bad things. Yet there was one man who found

127

favor with God. Who was that? — It was Noah. Noah loved Jehovah God. He was never too busy to listen to God. Isn't that the way we should be too? —

One day Jehovah told Noah that He was going to destroy all people who kept on doing bad things. God was going to make it rain so much that the water would cover the whole earth, even the mountains.

Would Noah die too when all that water fell? — No; Jehovah was going to save him. Jehovah told Noah to build a big ark. An ark is like a boat, but it looks more like a big, long box or chest. It floats on the water. God told Noah to build the ark big enough so that he and his family and many of the animals would be safe inside it.

Now, Noah had never built an ark before. But God told him how to do it. Noah and his family worked very hard. They cut down large trees. With the wood from these trees they began putting the ark together. This took many, many years, because the ark was so large.

Did Jehovah give other people a chance to get into the ark and be saved? — Yes, he did. Jehovah told Noah to preach. So during all the years that the ark was being built, Noah warned the people about the coming flood.

Did any of them listen? — Only Noah' family did. All the rest were just too busy doing other things. They did not think they were

so bad, and they did not take time to listen.

Finally, all the animals that Jehovah wanted to save were brought into the ark. Now it was time for the people to get into the ark too. Noah and his family went inside. Then Jehovah shut the door. It was too late for anyone else to get in.

People outside still did not believe that the flood would come. But all of a sudden water began to fall! Noah had been right!

It was not just a regular rain. It was a downpour! Soon the water was like big rivers, making a lot of noise. It pushed over big trees and rolled big stones as if they were little pebbles.

What about the people outside the ark? — Jesus says: "The flood came and swept them all away." Even if they climbed a hill, that didn't help. The downpour didn't stop for forty days and forty nights. Soon the whole earth was covered with water. All the people outside the ark were now dead. Why? — As Jesus said, 'They did not listen!'

But there floating on the water was the ark. Noah, his family and the animals were safe inside. Jehovah saved the people who listened to Him.—Genesis 6:5–7:24.

Now, why should we know about what happened in Noah's day? Do you remember what Jesus said? — He said that what happened then is a lesson for us. Jehovah will again destroy all bad people, but this time he will not use a flood. The time for him to do this is near.

When God does this, who will be the people that God will keep alive? — Will it be persons who were so busy with other things that they never wanted to learn about God? Will it be persons who were always too busy to study the Bible? — Will it be those who never wanted to go to meetings where people learned God's will? What do you think? —

We want to be among those people whom God will keep alive, don't we? — Wouldn't it be wonderful if our family could be like Noah's so that God would save all of us? — Let's always help one another to be faithful to God so that he will save all of us.

(We need to make time in our lives to listen to God. Read what is said about this at Hosea 4:6, Matthew 13:18-22 and Deuteronomy 30:15, 16.)

32

"Happy Are the Peaceable"

DO YOU know any boys who are always trying to act big and tough? — Do you like to be with them? Or would you rather be with someone who is peaceable? —

The Great Teacher knows what kind of person God likes. He said: "Happy are the peaceable, since they will be called 'sons of God.' " That is the kind of person we want to be, isn't it? — We want to be peaceable.—Matthew 5:9.

But sometimes other people do things that make us angry. And we may feel like getting even with them. Once this happened to Jesus' disciples.

They were traveling with Jesus toward Jerusalem. When they had gone some distance, Jesus sent certain ones ahead to a village to find a place for them to rest. But the people there did not want them to stay. Those people had a different religion. And they did not like anyone that went to the city of Jerusalem to worship.

If that had happened to you, what would you have done? Would you have gotten angry? Would you have wanted to get even with them? —

That is what the disciples James and John wanted to do. They said to Jesus: 'Do you want us to tell fire to come down from heaven and destroy them?' But Jesus told them it was not right to treat other people that way.—Luke 9:51-56.

It is true that people may be mean to us at times. Other children may not want you to play in their games. They may even say, "We don't want you around here." When something like that happens, it can make us feel bad, can't it? — We may feel like doing something to get even with them. But should we? —

Why not get your copy of the Bible? And let's turn to Proverbs chapter twenty-four, verse twenty-nine. There it reads: "Do not say: 'Just as he did to me, so I am going to do to him. I shall repay to each one according to his acting.' "

What does that mean to you? — It is saying that we should not try to get even. We should not be mean to the other person because he was mean to us. God does not want us to do that.

But what if someone tries to pick a fight with you? He may try to get you angry by calling you names. He may laugh at you and say that you're scared. Maybe he calls you a sissy. What should you do? Should you let yourself be drawn into a fight? —

Again, let's see what the Bible says. Turn to Matthew chapter five and verse thirty-nine. There Jesus says: "Do not resist him that is wicked; but whoever slaps you on your right cheek, turn the other also to him."

What did Jesus mean by that? Did he mean that if someone hits you with his fist on one side of your face, you should let him hit you on the other side? — No, he did not mean that.

A slap is not like a hit with the fist. It is more like a push or a shove. A person does this to pick a fight. He wants us to get angry. And if we do get angry and push or shove back, what happens? — We will probably get into a fight.

Jesus did not want his followers to act like that. So he said that if someone slaps us, we should not slap back. We should not become angry and get into a fight. If we do, we show that we are no better than the one who started the fight.

If trouble starts, the best thing is to walk away. The other fellow may push or shove a few more times. But that will probably be the end of it. When you walk away, it does not show that you are weak. It shows that you are strong for what is right.

Now, what should we do if we see other people fighting? Should we get in there and take sides with one or the other? —

The Bible tells us what is right. Turn to Proverbs chapter twenty-six and verse seventeen It says: "As one grabbing hold of the ears of a dog is anyone passing by that is becoming furious at the quarrel that is not his."

What would happen if you grabbed hold of the ears of a dog? It would hurt the dog, and he would snap at you, wouldn't he? — The more the dog tried to get loose, the harder you would squeeze the ears. And the more excited the dog would get. If you let him go, he would probably bite you hard. But can you just stand there and hold his ears forever? —

Well, that is the kind of trouble that we would be in if we got mixed up in a fight between other people. We may not know who started the fight or why they are fighting. One person may be getting beaten, but perhaps he stole something from the other one. If we helped him, we would be helping a thief. That would not be good, would it? —

So, what should you do if you see a fight? — If it is at school, you can run and tell a teacher. And if it is away from school, you can call a policeman.

Even when other people want to fight, we can be peaceable. They may want to fight. But we can show that we are strong for what is right.

(More good counsel that can help a person stay out of fights is found at Romans 12:17-21, Psalm 34:14 [33:15, Dy] and 2 Timothy 2:24.)

134

33

"Caesar's Things to Caesar"

LET'S take out some money and look at it. What do you see on the money? — Who made this money? — The government did.

For thousands of years governments have made the money that people use. When the Great Teacher was on earth, the Roman government made money. And do you know who the ruler of that government was? — He was called Caesar.

The Roman government did many good things for the people in those days. And governments today do many good things for us. They build roads for travel. They pay policemen and firemen to protect us.

It costs money for a government to do these things. Do you know where the government gets the money? — It gets it from the people. The money that people pay to the government is called taxes.

Many people do not like to pay taxes. When Jesus was on earth, some of the Jews did not want to pay any taxes to the Roman government. They hated such taxes. So, one day some men came to the Great Teacher and asked him: 'Do we have to pay taxes to Caesar or not?'

Now, the men asked this question to trick

Jesus. For if Jesus answered, 'Yes, you must pay taxes,' many of the Jews would not like what Jesus said. But Jesus could not say, 'No, you don't need to pay taxes.' It would be wrong to say that.

So this is what Jesus did. He said to those men: 'Show me a coin.' When they brought him a coin, Jesus asked them: 'Whose picture and name are on it?'

The men said: "Caesar's."

So Jesus said: "By all means, then, pay back Caesar's things to Caesar, but God's things to God."—Luke 20:19-26.

Wasn't that a fine answer? — No one could find anything wrong with that. If Caesar does things for people, it is only right to use the money that Caesar made to pay him for these things. So in this way Jesus showed that it is right to pay taxes to the government for the things we receive.

Now, you may not be old enough to pay taxes. But there is something that you should give to the government. Do you know what that is? — It is obedience to the government's laws.

It is God who tells us this. His Word says: 'Be obedient

to the superior authorities.' And who are the 'superior authorities'? — The men who have power in the government. So we really should obey the law. God says so.—Romans 13:1, 2.

Consider an example. There may be a law not to throw paper or other litter on the street. Should you obey that law? — Yes, God wants you to obey it.

Should we be obedient to policemen too? — The government pays policemen to protect people. Obeying them is the same as obeying the government.

So if you are about to cross a street and a policeman says, "Wait!" what should you do? — What if others run across anyway, should you? — Even if you are the only one who waits, you should. God tells us to obey.

There may be trouble in the neighborhood and a policeman may say, "Stay off the streets. Don't go outside." But you may hear shouting and wonder what's going on. Should you go outside to see? — Would this be obeying the 'superior authorities'? —

The government in many places also builds schools. And it pays the teachers. When the children do what the teacher says, it makes for peace in the classroom. So do you think God wants you to obey the teacher? —

137

There is no scripture in the Bible that says, "Obey your teacher." But the Bible shows that you should obey. The government pays the teacher to teach, just as it pays a policeman to protect people. So being obedient to either a policeman or a teacher is like obeying the government.

Or we can look at it this way. God tells children to 'obey their father and mother.' But your father and mother have sent you to school for the teacher to look after you. So it is right to obey your teacher, just as you obey your parents at home.—Ephesians 6:1.

I am not always with you. So I may not see whether you obey the teacher. But God sees. And it is God whom we really want to please, isn't it? — Also, I may not see if you obey the policeman. But who does see? — God does. Always remember that.

Remember, too, that God comes first in our lives. We obey the government because that is what God wants us to do. But what if they tell us to do what God says we should not do? — If anyone tells us, "You don't have to obey God," does God want us to listen to that? —

That happened to the apostles of Jesus. Now what would the apostles do? What would you have done? — They answered: "We must obey God as ruler rather than men."—Acts 5:29.

(Respect for the law is taught in the Bible. Read what is written at Titus 3:1, Matthew 5:41 and 1 Peter 2:12-14.)

34

Worship Belongs to God

I AM going to ask you an important question. It is so important that the way you answer affects your future life. Who is your God? —

Your God is the one you worship. People all over the earth worship many kinds of gods. Some of those gods are simply carved or made from wood or stone. Others are people well known in sports or music. They are spoken of as "stars" and "idols." But is it right to give glory to these other gods? —

The Great Teacher said: "It is Jehovah your God you must worship, and it is to him alone you must render sacred service."—Matthew 4:10.

So Jesus made it clear. Our worship belongs only to Jehovah God. We cannot give even a little bit of our worship to any other god. There is a thrilling story in the Bible about some young men who knew this.

Their names were Shadrach, Meshach and Abednego. They were Hebrews, but they lived in the land of Babylon. The king of Babylon built a huge image of gold. He commanded that when the music was played, everyone should bow down to his image. 'Whoever does not bow down and worship will at that same moment be thrown into the burning fiery furnace,' he warned. What would you have done? —

Shadrach, Meshach and Abednego usually did everything that the king commanded. But they refused to do this. Do you know why? — It is because God's law said: 'You must not have any other gods besides me. You must not make for yourself a carved image and bow down to it.' So Shadrach, Meshach and Abednego obeyed the law of Jehovah rather than the command of the king.—Exodus 20:3, 4.

The king was very angry when he heard about this. Right away he had Shadrach, Meshach and Abednego brought before him. He asked: 'Is it really so that you are not serving my own gods? I will give you another chance. Now, when you hear the music, fall down and worship the image I have made. If you do not, you will be thrown into the burning fiery furnace. And who is that god that can rescue you out of my hands?'

What would Shadrach, Meshach and Abednego do now? What would you have done? — They trusted in Jehovah. They spoke right up and said to the king: 'Our God whom we are serving is able to rescue us. But even if he does not do it, your gods are not the ones we will serve. We will not bow down to your image of gold.'

The king was furious. He commanded: 'Let the furnace be heated seven times hotter than usual!' He ordered his strong men to tie up

Shadrach, Meshach and Abednego. Then he said: 'Throw them into the furnace!'

The king's servants threw them in. But the furnace was so hot that the king's own men were killed by the flames! What about the three Hebrews?

Shadrach, Meshach and Abednego fell right into the middle of the fire. But then they got up! They were not hurt. And no longer were they tied up. How could this be possible?

The king looked into the furnace, and what he saw made him afraid. 'Did we not throw three men into the fire?' he asked.

His servants answered: 'Yes, O king.'

But the king said: 'Look! I see four men walking about in there, and the fire is not hurting any of them.'

Do you know who that fourth person was? — It was Jehovah's angel. And he was there to protect those three

faithful Hebrew servants of the true God.

On seeing this, the king came to the door of the furnace and cried out: "Shadrach, Meshach and Abednego, you servants of the Most High God, step out and come here!" When they came out, everyone could see that they had not been burned. There was not even the smell of fire on them.

Then the king said: 'Blessed be the God of Shadrach, Meshach and Abednego who saved his servants, because they would not worship any god at all except their own God.'—Daniel chapter three.

Wasn't that wonderful? — Jehovah was pleased with what those three young men did. And we can learn a lesson from it.

Even today men set up images for worship. Some are made of wood or stone or metal. Would you bow to these images? —

Other images are made of cloth. Have you ever seen that kind of image? — Do you think it makes a difference to God if it is made out of cloth or out of wood or stone? — Would it be right for a servant of Jehovah to do an act of worship before such an image? —

Shadrach, Meshach and Abednego would give worship only to Jehovah. God was pleased with them. Will you copy their example? —

(Those who serve Jehovah cannot also worship images. Read what is said about this at Isaiah 42:8 and Joshua 24:14, 15, 19-22.)

35

"More Happiness in Giving"

I KNOW a secret. Would you like to hear it? — It is the secret of happiness.

There are a lot of people who are not happy. Some depend too much on what other people do. If someone gives them something nice, they are happy. If no one does something special for them, they are not happy.

Now, here is the secret. The Great Teacher said: "There is more happiness in giving than there is in receiving." So, the one who is most happy is not the person who gets things, but the one who gives to other people. Did you know that? — —Acts 20:35.

Just think about what it means. Did Jesus say that a person who received a gift would not be happy? — No. You like to get gifts, don't you? — And so do I. We are happy when we receive nice things.

But Jesus said that there is even more happiness when we give. And Jesus was always right, wasn't he? —

Now, what is there that we can give to other people? What would you say? —

Sometimes when you want to give a gift, it costs money. At least, if it is a gift that you get in a store, you will have to pay for it. So, if you

143

 want to give that kind of gift, you may have to save money until you get enough to buy the gift.

But not all gifts come from stores. Let me explain. On a hot day there is nothing as good as a cold glass of fresh water. You don't have to go to the store for it. Yet when you give it to someone who is thirsty, you can have the happiness that comes from giving.

Someday maybe you and your mother can bake some cookies. That can be fun. And when they first come out of the oven, they taste specially good. But what might we do with some of those cookies that would make us even happier than eating all of them ourselves? —

Yes, the greater happiness comes from giving. We can have a good time eating some ourselves. But, if we want even more happiness, then we might wrap up some of them and make a gift of them to one of our friends. Would you like to do that sometime? —

The apostle Paul was one who knew the happiness of giving. What did he give to other people? — He had the best thing in the world to give. He knew the truth about God and about Jesus. Gladly he shared it with others. And he did it without letting anyone give him money for his help.

144

One time the apostle Paul and his companion Luke met a woman who also wanted to have the happiness of giving. They met her down by a river. Paul and Luke had gone there because they heard that it was a place of prayer. And sure enough, they found some women there.

Paul began to tell these women the good things about Jehovah God and his kingdom. One of them named Lydia paid close attention. She liked very much what she heard. And she wanted to do something to show her appreciation.

Luke tells us: 'She urged us: "If you men have judged me to be faithful to Jehovah, enter into my house and stay." And she just made us come.' —Acts 16:11-15.

Lydia was glad to have these servants of God in her home. She loved them because they had helped her to learn about God's way for people to live forever. It made her happy to be able to give them food to eat and a place to rest.

So, Lydia's giving made her happy because she really wanted to give. And that is something that we ought to remember. Someone may tell us to give a gift. But if we really don't want to do it, then the giving will not make us happy.

For example, what if you had a bar of candy that you wanted to eat? If I told you that you had to give it to another child, would it make you happy to give it away? — But you may have a bar of candy when you meet a friend that you like very much. If you got the idea all by yourself that it would be nice to split the candy bar with your friend, then you would be happy about doing it, wouldn't you? —

And, do you know that sometimes we love a person so much that we want to give him everything, and not keep back anything for ourselves? As we grow in love, that is the way we should feel toward God.

The Great Teacher knew a woman who felt that way. He saw her in the temple in Jerusalem. She had just two small coins; that is all she had. But she put both of them in the box as a contribution or a gift for the temple. No one made her do it. She did it because she wanted to, because she really loved God. It made her happy to be able to give.

So, there are many ways in which we can give, aren't there? — And the Great Teacher knows that if we give because we want to, we will be happy. That is why he tells us: "Practice giving." That is, make it a habit to give to other people. If we do that, we will not be sad because of waiting for someone else to do something nice for us. We will be busy making other people happy. And when we do that, we are the happiest ones of all!—Luke 6:38.

(More fine thoughts as to the kind of giving that brings happiness are found at Matthew 6:1-4, 2 Corinthians 9:7 and Luke 14:12-14.)

36

The Boastful Pharisee

WHAT does it mean to be boastful? Do you know? —

Here is an example. Have you ever tried to do something that you are not very good at? Maybe you tried to hit a baseball. Or maybe you tried to skip rope. Did anyone ever say, "Ha! Ha! Ha! I can do that better than you can"? — Well, that person was boasting. He was bragging about himself.

How do you feel when others do that? Do you like it? — Then, how do you think others would feel when you boast? — Is it kind to tell someone else, "I'm better than you"? — Does Jehovah like people who do that? —

The Great Teacher knew some people who did things like that. One day he told them a story. It was about a Pharisee and a tax collector.

The Pharisees were proud religious teachers. They often acted as if they were more righteous or holier than other people. The Pharisee in Jesus' story went up to God's temple in Jerusalem to pray.

Jesus said that a tax collector also went up there to pray. Now, most people did not like tax collectors. They felt that the tax collectors were against them. And, besides that, some tax collectors were not always honest.

At the temple the Pharisee began praying to God this way: 'O God, I thank you that I am not a sinner like other people. I do not cheat people or do other bad things. I am not like that tax collector over there. I am a righteous man. I go without food twice a week so that I have more time to think about you. And I give to the temple a tenth of all the things that I get.' That Pharisee really thought he was righteous, didn't he? — And he told God about it too.

But the tax collector was not like that. He did not feel that he was good enough even to come close to God's temple. He would not even raise his eyes toward heaven. So he kept standing at a distance with his head bowed. He was sorry about his sins. And he hit his chest in grief. He did not try to tell God how good he was. But he prayed: 'O God, be kind to me a sinner.'

Which of those men do you think was pleasing to God? Was it the boastful Pharisee, the one who thought he was so good? Or was it the tax collector, who felt sorry about his sins? —

Jesus said: 'To God, the tax collector was more righteous than the Pharisee. Because everyone who tries to make it look as if he is better than other people will be brought low. But he that is lowly in his own eyes will be raised up.'—Luke 18:9-14.

Did you get the lesson that Jesus was teaching? — He was showing that it is wrong to think that we are better than other people. Let's see how this lesson fits our lives.

Perhaps you and another child are being asked some questions at school. What if you are able to give the answers right away, but the other child is slower? Of course, you feel good when you know the answers. But would it be kind to tell the other student that he is dumb? — Is it right to try to make yourself look good by making the other person look bad? —

That is what the Pharisee did. He bragged that he was better than the tax collector. But the Great Teacher said that he was wrong.

It is true that one person may be able to do a certain thing better than someone else. But does that mean that he is a better person? —

Think about it. If we know a lot, should we boast? — Did we make our own brain? — No, God is the One who gave man a brain. And

all the things we know we learned from someone else. Maybe we read it in a book. Or perhaps someone told us. Even if we figured it out by ourselves, how did we do it? By looking at things that God had made. Everything we have came from someone else.

Some people are strong. Does that make them better than everyone else? — They did not make their own bodies, did they? — God is the One who gave muscles to man. And God is the One who makes food grow so that we can eat and be strong.

So, do any of us have reason to boast? Are we better than other people? — Instead of telling others how good we are, we should really be telling them how wonderful Jehovah is, shouldn't we? — Because he is the One who makes it possible for us to do things well.

When a person tries hard, the kind thing is to say something that makes him feel good. Tell him that you like what he did. Maybe you can even help him to do better. That is what you would like people to do for you, isn't it? — Well, Jesus said: 'Just as you want other people to do to you, do the same way to them.' That is a good rule to follow, isn't it? — —Luke 6:31.

If we do that, we will never brag or boast. We won't be like that boastful Pharisee.

(Pride and bragging are things to be avoided. Read what these scriptures say: Proverbs 16:5, 18; 1 Corinthians 4:7; 13:4.)

37

The Apostle Who Became a Thief

HAS anyone ever stolen anything from you? — How did you feel about it? — Whoever stole it was a thief, and nobody likes a thief.

Did you know that one of Jesus' apostles became a thief? — His name was Judas Iscariot.

Judas knew the things it was right to do. Even when he was a small boy he had heard the law of God. He knew that once God had even spoken from heaven with a big voice and told his people: "You must not steal." Judas knew that God's law was right.—Exodus 20:15.

When he grew up he met the Great Teacher. Judas liked the things that Jesus said. Judas became a disciple of Jesus. Later, Jesus even picked Judas to be one of his twelve apostles.

Jesus and his apostles spent much time together. They traveled together. They ate together. And money for the group was kept together in a box. Jesus gave that box to Judas to take care of.

Of course, the money did not belong to Judas. Jesus was the one who would tell him how to use it. But do you know what Judas did after a while? He started to take money from the box when he wasn't supposed to. He would take it when the others were not looking. He became a thief. Now he began to think about money all the time. He tried to find ways to get more of it.

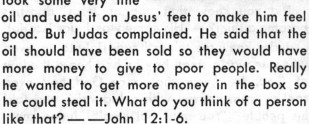

One day a woman took some very fine oil and used it on Jesus' feet to make him feel good. But Judas complained. He said that the oil should have been sold so they would have more money to give to poor people. Really he wanted to get more money in the box so he could steal it. What do you think of a person like that? — —John 12:1-6.

Jesus did not tell Judas right then that he was a thief. But he did tell him not to make trouble for the woman who had been so kind. Judas did not like that. What would he do?

He should have felt sorry. He should have told Jesus that he had been stealing, and he should have put the money back. But, instead, he did something terrible.

He went to the chief priests, who were enemies of Jesus. They wanted to arrest Jesus. But they wanted to do it at night so people would not see them. Judas told them: 'I will tell you how you can get Jesus, if you give me money. How much will you give me?' The priests said: 'We will give you thirty pieces of silver!' That was a lot of money.—Matthew 26:14-16.

Wicked Judas took the money. It was just as if he was selling the Great Teacher to those men. Can you imagine anyone doing such a terrible thing? — Well, that is the kind of thing that happens when a person becomes a thief. He loves money more than he loves God.

Now, let's be sure that we understand this matter clearly. To understand what a thief is, we need to know what it means to own something. People own things because they have worked for them. Or they bought them with money. Or maybe they were given to them as gifts.

When your father works he gets paid money for it. Does he own that money? — Yes, because he worked for it. It is not yours; it is his.

With that money he buys the things in your home. He owns them. Because he owns them, he has the right to say who may use them. He tells you if you can play with them or not. And he probably lets your mother tell you this too.

Sometimes you go to play with other children in their house, don't you? — The things in their house belong to their father. Would it be all right to take something from their house and carry it to your house? — Not unless their father or mother tells you that you can. If you carry something home without asking them, that would be stealing.

Why does a person steal? — Well, he may see something that belongs to another person. Perhaps it is a bicycle. The more he looks at that bicycle and thinks about it, the more he likes it. If he is not a loving person, he does not care how the other person feels. So he may hit the other person and try to take the bicycle away from him. Or he may wait until the other person is not looking. Then he takes the bicycle away. What is he really doing? — He is stealing.

Maybe the other person doesn't see him steal the bicycle. But someone sees him do it. Do you know who? — Jehovah God sees him do it. God sees that he is a thief.

It does not make any difference if the other person has many things or just a few. Some people go to a store and see lots of things there. They see something that they want very much. They may tell themselves that nobody will miss just one. So they take it, but they do not pay for it. Is that right? — No, it is stealing.

When people do that, they are being like Judas. Because Judas was a thief! Let's be sure that we are never like him.

(It is wrong to steal. The Bible makes this clear at Mark 10:17-19; Romans 13:9; Ephesians 4:28.)

38

Love for God's House

DO YOU like it when we are invited to go to someone's house for dinner? — What if we were invited to God's house, would you want to go? —

Now, you may say that God does not live in a house. And it is true that God does not live in a house in the way that we do.

But the Great Teacher said that God had a "house." And Jesus used to go to God's house, even when he was a little boy. That house was the beautiful temple of Jehovah in the city of Jerusalem. That temple belonged to God. It was used for his worship. So it was called "the house of Jehovah."

When Jesus was a boy, he lived a long way from the "house of Jehovah." No one had a car in those days, and there were no trains that they could ride. To get to the temple, they would have to walk. It was not a trip of just an hour or so from where they lived. They would have to walk for at least three days to get there. And the return trip would take another three days. Was it worth all the effort to make such a trip? Would you have walked that far to spend time in "God's house"? —

People who loved "God's house" did not

155

think it was too far. Every year Jesus' parents would go to Jerusalem to worship. And Jesus went with them.

One year, as they began the trip home, Jesus was not with his family. No one noticed it until they had traveled a long way. Then his parents went back to hunt for him. And where do you suppose he was? —

They found him right in the temple. He was listening to the teachers. He was asking questions. And when they asked him something, he would answer. They were amazed at the fine answers that he gave.

Of course, when his parents finally found him, they felt much better. But Jesus had not been worried. He knew that the temple was a good place to be. So he asked: "Did you not know that I must be in the house of my Father?" He knew that the temple was "God's house." And he loved to be there.—Luke 2:41-49.

It was not just once a year that Jesus and his parents went to meetings for worship. Each week there were meetings for worship in the town where they lived.

At those meetings someone would get up and read from the Bible. They did not have it all in one book. It was written on long scrolls or rolls. So they would unroll it to the place that they wanted and then start to read. After that it would be explained. The Bible says that it was Jesus' "custom" to attend these meetings. That means that he went regularly.—Luke 4:16.

We should do that too. But where is "God's house" today? Where should we go to worship him? —

The temple where Jesus went in Jerusalem is no longer there. It was destroyed. So we can't go there.

But God still does have a "house." It is not a house that is made of stones. It is made up of people. How could that be? Well, a house is a place to live. And God says that he is with his people. He does not leave heaven and come down to the earth. But God is so close to his people that they feel as if he were right there with them.—1 Peter 2:5; Ephesians 2:22; 1 Timothy 3:15.

So, when we go to "God's house," where should we go? — We should go where God's people have met for worship. It could be in a big building. It could be in a small one. Or it could be in someone's home. The important thing is that they really be God's people. But how can we tell if they are his people? —

Well, what do they do at their meetings? Do

they really teach what is in the Bible? Do they read it and discuss it? That is how we listen to God, isn't it? — And at "God's house" we would expect to hear what God says, wouldn't we? —

But what if people say that you do not have to live the way the Bible says? Would you say that they are God's people? —

Here is something else to think about. The Bible says that God's people would be "a people for his name." What is God's name? — It is Jehovah. So we can ask people if their God is Jehovah. If they say "No," then we know that they are not his people.—Acts 15:14.

But it is not enough just to say that Jehovah is their God. Where is the proof? They should be talking about him to other people. They should be telling people about God's kingdom. They should have faith in his Son. They should show their love for God by keeping his commandments.—Isaiah 43:10.

Do we know people who do all those things? — Then we should be meeting with them for worship. And we should be there regularly. We should be listening to those who teach, and answering questions when they are asked. That is what Jesus did when he was in "God's house." If we do that, we show that we, too, really love the "house of God."

(We should take pleasure in regularly attending meetings with God's people. Read what is said about this at Psalm 122:1 [121:1, Dy]; Hebrews 10:23-25.)

39

'Blessed Is the One
Coming as King'

DO YOU know the Lord's Prayer? — Let me hear you say it. — If you don't remember it, we will read it together from the Bible at Matthew chapter six, verses nine to thirteen.

Now, in that prayer it says, "Let your kingdom come." What is a kingdom? Do you know? —

A kingdom is a government. And you know what that is, don't you? — The government is a group of persons who rule a country.

In a government there is a head person or ruler. In some countries this person is called the president. But do you know what the ruler of God's government is called? — He is the king.

For God's kingdom Jehovah himself has picked the king. Do you know who that king is? — He is Jesus Christ. He is better than any ruler that men choose. Jesus has more power than any of those rulers. And Jesus really loves God, so he always does what is right.

Long ago in Israel new kings would ride into Jerusalem on a colt to show themselves to the people. This is what Jesus did.

Just outside of Jerusalem there was a small village. As Jesus got near to it, he said to two of his disciples: 'Go into that village, and you

159

will find a colt. Loose it and bring it to me.'

The disciples did just as Jesus said. And when they brought the colt to Jesus, he sat down upon it. As he got near Jerusalem, a great crowd of people came out to meet him.

As Jesus rode along, most of the crowd began laying their outer garments on the road in front of him. Others cut down branches from the trees and put these on the road. They showed by this that they wanted Jesus as king.

The people were glad to welcome Jesus. They cried out: "Blessed is the One coming as the King in Jehovah's name!"

But not everyone was happy that Jesus was riding into Jerusalem as king. Some even said to Jesus, 'Tell your disciples to be quiet.'—Luke 19:28-40.

How do you feel about having Christ as king? — If you had been living when Jesus rode into Jerusalem, would you have welcomed him

as the one sent by Jehovah to his people? —

Well, Jesus is not on earth today, is he? — He is in heaven. It is from there in heaven that he rules as king. Even though we cannot see him, he can see every one of us here on earth. We can't fool him. He sees what we do, and he even knows what we are thinking. If we really love Jehovah, he knows that. And if we are trying hard to do what the Bible says, he will help us. Would you like to have him as your king forever? —

Not everyone wants Christ to be king. They may say they believe in God, but they do not want his kingdom. They don't want God or Christ to be telling them what to do. They want their own governments right here on earth. So do you know what is going to happen to them? —

The Bible gives us the answer at Daniel chapter two, verse forty-four. Let's get our Bibles and turn there together. This scripture is speaking about our own day when it says: "In the days of those kings the God of heaven will set up a kingdom that will never be brought to ruin. And the kingdom itself will not be passed on to any other people. It will crush and put an end to all these kingdoms, and it itself will stand to times indefinite."

Did you understand that? — The Bible says that God's government is going to destroy all these earthly governments. Why? — Because they don't obey the one whom God has made king.

The whole earth belongs to God. He made it as well as the whole universe. So he has the right to decide what kind of government should rule. And his government is the best. Soon God's kingdom will be the only government there is.

Do you want to live forever under God's kingdom? — I do. But we need to prove that to God. Do you know how? — It is by learning the laws of God and obeying them every day.

Now, God says that his kingdom will destroy the governments of men. But does he tell us that we should do that? — No. The Bible says that we should obey the laws of men, just as long as God lets those governments rule.

But if we really want Christ as king, we have to do more than that. We have to obey all the things that Christ said. He said that we should be "no part of the world." Would we be obeying him if we tried to be a part of the governments of the world? — Jesus and his apostles stayed away from such things.—John 17:14.

What did they do instead? — They talked to other people about God's kingdom. That was the big work in their lives. Can we do that too? — Yes, and we will do it if we mean what we say when we pray for God's kingdom to come.

(Take a few more minutes now to read these further scriptures that show how we should view the one whom God has made king: Isaiah 9:6, 7; Daniel 7:13, 14; John 18:36; Matthew 6:33.)

40

Jesus Gave His Life for Us

YOU have some good friends, don't you? —
But suppose they were in real danger. What
if they were in a boat that was sinking? Would
you want to save them if you could? — Would
you do it even if you might die yourself while
helping them? — A person who would give his
life to save other people shows that he loves
them very much.

Jesus proved he had that kind of love for us.
He was willing to leave heaven and to be sent
to earth to die for us. Did you know that he died
for us? —

Would you like to hear how he did this? —
Let's pretend that we are right there and can see
what happens.

It is very late one spring night at Jerusalem.
The moon shines big and bright. As we look at
the city we see Jesus and his apostles walk
through a big gate and leave the city. They come
to a hill that is called the Mount of Olives and
go into a garden. Shall we follow them? —

As we watch, we see Jesus go away from his
disciples and kneel to pray to his Father. He does
this three times. And each time he comes back
and tells his disciples that they should be praying
too. Why? What is going to happen? —

163

Look! Do you see those men coming toward the garden? Some of them have lamps. Others have clubs. There are soldiers with swords. They look very unfriendly. Surely Jesus must see them coming. Shouldn't he try to run away? —

Jesus sees them, but he doesn't run. Now the soldiers come up and arrest Jesus. Will he let them take him away? He could call to his Father. God could send him thousands of angels. They could destroy those men in a couple of seconds. If you had been Jesus, would you have called for the angels? —

But Jesus lets the men take him. Why? — Because he is willing to die for us. There is an even more important reason. He tells the disciple Peter: 'God's Word must come true.' You see, it was already written in the Bible that Jesus would give his life for mankind.

Jesus' disciples now become afraid and run away. The soldiers take Jesus back to the city. Let's follow them and see what happens.

They take Jesus before the chief priests. These priests hate Jesus because he has been showing people that the priests do not teach the Bible.

The priests hold a trial. They bring in men who tell lies about Jesus. They ask Jesus questions to try to prove he has done something wrong. But they cannot prove a thing against him. Then the priests say to Jesus: 'Are you the Son of God?' Jesus says: 'I am.' The priests get angry and say: 'He's guilty! He should be killed!'

All the others agree. So some of the men there start making fun of Jesus. They spit on him and hit him with their fists. Does Jesus begin to feel sorry that he has taught the truth from the Bible? How would you have felt? —

Well, Jesus isn't sorry and he doesn't even complain or hit back.

Now morning comes. Jesus has been up all night. The priests now have Jesus bound, and they lead him to Pilate, the governor.

They tell Pilate: 'Jesus is against the government. He should be killed.' But Pilate can see that the priests are telling lies. So Pilate tells them: 'I find nothing wrong with this man. I will let him go.' But the priests and others shout: 'No! Kill him!'

Later, Pilate tries again to tell the people he is going to let Jesus go free. But the priests get the crowds to shout: 'If you let him go you are against the government too! Kill him!' It becomes very noisy. What will Pilate do?

He gives in. First he has Jesus whipped. Then he turns him over to soldiers to be put to death.

They give Jesus a big post or stake to carry. Finally they get to a spot called Skull Place outside the city. There they nail Jesus' hands and feet to the stake. Then they stand it up so that Jesus is hanging on it. He is bleeding. The pain is very great.

Jesus does not die right away. He just hangs there on the stake. The chief priests make fun of him. They say: "If you are a son of God, come down off the torture stake!" But Jesus knows what his Father has sent him to do. He knows that he must give his perfect life so that we can have the chance to get everlasting life. Finally, about three o'clock that afternoon, Jesus cries out to his Father and dies.—Matthew 26:36–27:50; Luke 22:39–23:46; John 18:1–19:30.

How different Jesus was from Adam! Adam did not show love for God. He disobeyed God. Neither did Adam show love for us. Because he sinned, all of us have been born with sin in us. But Jesus showed love for God and for us. He obeyed God always. And he gave his life so that he could take away the harm that Adam did to us.

Do you appreciate what a wonderful thing Jesus did? — When you pray to God, do you thank him for what his Son did? — That will show you appreciate it. And if we really do what the Great Teacher says, we will show even more how much we appreciate that he gave his life for us.

(To build appreciation for what Jesus did for us, read John 3:16; Romans 5:8, 19; 1 Timothy 2:5, 6; Matthew 20:28.)

41

A Meal to Help Us Remember

SUPPOSE someone gave you a wonderful gift. How would you feel about it? — Would you just say, "Thank you," and then forget all about the one who gave it to you? Or would you want to remember what he did? —

Jehovah has given a very wonderful gift to us. He sent his own Son to earth to die for us. Because of this we can get free from sickness and death. What a loving thing for them to do! Surely we do not want to forget what God and his Son have done for us, do we? —

Did you know that God's Son gave us a special way to remember what he did? — Would you like to hear about it? —

Just imagine you are in the upstairs room of a house in Jerusalem. It is nighttime. Let us see who is in the room. The Great Teacher is there. So are his apostles. They are lying on couches around a table. On the table there is some roast lamb, flat loaves of bread and red wine. But this is not a regular meal. They are having a special meal. Do you know why? —

This meal is to remind them of something very important that happened hundreds of years before. It was on the night when Jehovah set his people Israel free from slavery in Egypt.

Jehovah told his people: 'Kill a lamb for each family and put its blood on the doorposts of your houses.' Then he said: 'Go inside your houses and eat the lamb.'

They did that. And that same night God's angel passed through the land of Egypt. In most houses the angel killed the firstborn child. But when the angel saw blood on the doorposts, he passed over that house. In those houses no children died. If you had been there, in which of the houses would you have wanted to be? —

The king of Egypt was frightened by what Jehovah's angel did. He told the Israelites: 'You are free. Get out of Egypt!' So they loaded up their camels and donkeys and left.

But Jehovah did not want his people to forget how he set them free. So he said: 'Once a year you must eat a meal like the meal you ate tonight. And you should tell your children about what happened this night in Egypt.'

They called this special meal the Passover. Do you know why? — Because that night God's angel had 'passed over' their houses marked with blood. Remember?

Jesus and his apostles are thinking about this when they eat the Passover meal. Afterward Jesus does something very important. Watch carefully.

He picks up one of the leftover loaves of bread. After praying over it, he breaks it. He passes it to his disciples and says: "Take, eat."

Then he tells them: 'This bread stands for my body that I will give when I die for you.'

Next Jesus picks up a cup of red wine. After another prayer of thanks, he passes it around. He says: "Drink out of it, all of you." And he tells them: 'This wine stands for my blood. Soon I am going to pour out my blood to free you from your sins. Keep doing this to remember me.' —Matthew 26:26-28; 1 Corinthians 11:23-26.

Did you notice that Jesus said they should keep doing this to remember him? — No longer would they have the Passover meal. Instead, once each year they would have this special meal to remember Jesus' death. This is called the Lord's evening meal. Today we also call it the Memorial. Why? — Because it brings back to our memory what Jesus and his Father have done for us.

Will you go with me to the Memorial next time it is held? — If you do, you will see some flat bread and red wine being passed around. What will the bread and wine make you think of? —

The bread should make us think of Jesus' body. He was willing to give up that body so that we could have everlasting life. And what about the red wine? — That should remind us of Jesus' blood that was poured out when men nailed him to a stake to die.

Jesus' blood is much more precious than the blood of the passover lamb in Egypt. Do you know why? — Jesus' blood can bring us forgiveness of sins.

Do you know what it will mean to have all our sins taken away? — Then we will never do anything wrong again. And we will no longer get sick, grow old and die! We should think of that when we go to the Memorial.

Should everyone eat the bread and drink the wine at the Memorial? — No, Jesus told those who do: 'You will have part in my kingdom and sit on thrones in heaven with me.' That meant they would go to heaven to be kings with Jesus. Only those who are going to do that should take the bread and wine.

But even if we do not eat the bread or drink the wine, we should attend the Memorial. Do you know why? — Because Jesus gave his life for us too. When we go to the Memorial we show that we have not forgotten. We remember God's wonderful gift through Jesus.

(Other scriptures to read to show the importance of attending the Memorial are Luke 22:19, 20, 28-30; 1 Corinthians 11:27.)

42

An Empty Tomb

DID the Great Teacher really die on the torture stake? — Yes, he did. Many persons saw it happen. Some even saw when a soldier came up and jabbed a spear into Jesus' side. They saw the blood run out. Yes, the Great Teacher was dead.

Later, a man named Joseph went to the Roman governor. Joseph believed in the Great Teacher. He said: 'Will you let me take Jesus' body down from the stake and bury it?' The governor said: 'Yes. Take it.' So Joseph carried Jesus' body to a garden where there was a tomb. Do you know what a tomb is? —

It is a place where dead bodies are put. Well, Jesus' body was put inside the tomb. Then a big round stone was rolled in front of the door of the tomb. The tomb was closed.

Jesus was dead. But Jesus had told his disciples that God would make him alive again. When? Jesus had said: 'On the third day after I die.' Is that what happened? Let's see.

It is very early in the morning, before sunrise. So it is still dark. Some soldiers are there guarding the tomb. The chief priests sent them to do that. Why? To keep Jesus' disciples away. But now something exciting happens.

Suddenly the ground begins to shake. In the darkness there is a flash of light. Look! It is an angel of Jehovah! The soldiers are so frightened they cannot move. The angel goes to the tomb. He rolls the stone away. Look inside. The tomb is empty!

Yes, Jehovah God has brought Jesus back to life. But He has made Jesus alive with a body like the one Jesus had before he came to earth. Do you remember what kind of body that was? — It was a body like the angels have, a spirit body.—1 Peter 3:18.

Can you see a spirit body? — No. So, if an angel wanted people to see him he had to make himself a body like ours. Then people could see him. Afterward the angel would disappear.

Now the sun is coming up. The soldiers have gone away. And some women who loved Jesus are coming to the tomb. They are asking themselves: 'Whom will we get to roll that heavy stone away for us?' But when they look, the stone has already been rolled away. And see, the tomb is empty! Jesus' dead body of flesh is gone! One of the women right away runs off to tell some of Jesus' apostles.

The other women stay by the tomb. They say: 'Where could Jesus' body be?' Suddenly two men in flashing clothing appear. They are angels! They say to the women: 'Why are you looking for Jesus here? He has been raised up. Go quickly and tell his disciples.'

Well, you can imagine how fast the women run! On the way a man meets them. Do you know who it is? — It is Jesus! He also says to the women: 'Go and tell my disciples.'

The women are excited. They find the disciples and tell them: 'Jesus is alive! We saw him!'

At first the disciples find this hard to believe. Still, they know the tomb is empty. Peter and John have been out there and seen that it is empty. The disciples want to believe that Jesus is alive again. But it seems too wonderful to be true. What will make them believe it? —

Later Jesus appears to some of those disciples. While two of them are walking along a road, Jesus starts walking with them. He talks to them and then disappears. He appears to Peter too.

Then later that same day many disciples are gathered in a room. The doors are locked, because they are afraid of the priests. Suddenly Jesus is right there in the room with them! Now they know the Great Teacher really is alive again. Imagine how happy they are!—Matthew 28:1-15; Luke 24:1-49; John 19:38—20:21.

After many days, Jesus leaves the earth and goes back to his Father in heaven. Soon the disciples start telling everyone that God raised

Jesus up from the dead. Many persons believe and become disciples.

This makes the chief priests angry. They have the apostles arrested. They tell them: 'Stop teaching the people these things!' They even have the apostles beaten with a whip. Do they stop teaching the people? What would you have done? —

The apostles do not stop. They are not afraid now. They are even willing to die if they have to. They know that God made Jesus alive again. They saw Jesus after he was raised from the dead. They are sure that God can make them alive too if they die faithful to him.—Acts 1:3-11; 5:40-42.

How different they were from many people today! Some people think only about Easter rabbits and colored Easter eggs when they think about Jesus' being raised up. But the Bible doesn't say anything about Easter rabbits and eggs. It talks about serving God.

We can be like Jesus' disciples. We can tell people what a wonderful thing God did when he made his Son alive again. We can obey God just as Jesus did. But what if we die because of obeying God, just as Jesus died? — We never need to be afraid. Jehovah can make us alive again under his righteous kingdom.

(Belief in Jesus' resurrection should give us a firm hope and make our faith strong. Read 1 Corinthians 15:3-8, 20-23; Acts 2:22-36; 4:18-20.)

43

Jesus Gives a Sign

TODAY we are going to talk about signs. It is good to know how to read signs. They can help us.

Some signs have words on them. They tell us where we can buy food. They may warn us not to cross the street when cars are coming. What signs have you seen? —

There are signs of another kind too. They may have no words. Some of them tell about changes in the weather. Clouds may cover the sun. Perhaps the wind starts to blow. Lightning flashes. There is thunder. When you hear and see these things, what do they mean? — Yes, there will probably be rain. It is not hard to read those signs, is it? —

One day Jesus' apostles asked him for a sign. They had heard him say that people would not see him again until some future time. They wanted to know when that time would be. What sign would there be that the time had come?

The Great Teacher knew that his followers would need a sign. He was going to go back to heaven to be with God. When he would come again he would not be a human. He would be a spirit. And can you see a spirit? —

So, how would anyone know that he had

175

come again? — Well, Jesus told them what to watch for. He told them about things that would happen right here on earth.

When Jesus was talking to them, they were close to Jerusalem. They could see it across the valley. And they could see its beautiful temple. So Jesus told them about things that would happen to Jerusalem and its temple. And those things did happen!

But Jesus also said that the same things would happen again later. This time they would happen to the whole world. And what would this mean? — It would mean that Christ had returned. It would mean that from heaven he had begun to rule in the kingdom of God. Soon he would destroy the wicked. Life would soon get much better here on earth.

Have we seen the sign that Jesus gave? — I have. Would you like to hear about it? —

As part of the sign, Jesus said: 'You are going to hear of wars and reports of wars. Nation will rise against nation and kingdom against kingdom.'

I have seen that in my lifetime. Whole nations have fought against other nations to destroy them. The trouble really began in the year 1914. Now we hear news reports about war almost every day. Have you heard those reports on the radio or on television? —

Here is another part of the sign that Jesus gave. He said: 'There will be food shortages in one place after another.'

Not everyone has enough food to eat. Did you know that? — I have heard that every day ten thousand people die because they do not have enough food. Lack of food also results in disease or pestilence. Jesus said that there would be food shortages and pestilence.

This is another part of the sign that he gave: 'There will be earthquakes in one place after another.'

Do you know what an earthquake is? — It makes the ground shake under your feet. Houses fall down and people often get killed. Since the year 1914 there have been many more earthquakes every year than there were before. These are things that have happened in my lifetime.

Jesus said that another part of the sign would be 'more and more lawlessness.' That is happening too. That is why people almost everywhere lock the door on their houses. They are afraid that someone might try to break in. And in many places it is not safe to walk on the street alone at night. Never before has it been as bad as it is now.—Matthew 23:39–24:22.

Some people may say that these things have happened before. But never before have they happened in so much of the world at the same time. All this has special meaning.

Remember, Jesus said that these things would be a sign. Can you read that sign? What does it mean? —

Most people see only the trouble. It makes them unhappy. But if they knew what the sign meant, they would rejoice. Why? —

Jesus said: 'As these things start to happen, lift your heads up, because your deliverance is getting near.' That means that we should be happy. Because in just a short time God will put an end to all the troubles on this earth. Life will be a real pleasure then.

Don't you agree that is good news? — If we really believe it, we won't keep it to ourselves. Other people need to know about it too.

(There is much in the Bible that shows that the time for God's kingdom has come. Read together these scriptures: Luke 21:28-36; 2 Timothy 3:1-5; 2 Peter 3:3, 4, 13.)

44

"You Will Be with Me in Paradise"

DO YOU like animals? — Would you like to be able to play with a lion? Or would you like to have a bear for a pet? —

The time is coming when you will be able to do that. Get your Bible and let's read about it together.

The scripture is in the book of Isaiah, chapter 11, verse 6. It says: "And the wolf will actually reside for a while with the male lamb, and with the kid the leopard itself will lie down, and the calf and the maned young lion and the well-fed animal all together; and a mere little boy will be leader over them."

What would happen today if a wolf could get at a lamb? — It would eat it up, wouldn't it? And what would happen if a leopard were with a little goat? — That little goat would become dinner for the leopard.

But the Bible says that is going to change. God is going to make those animals eat straw, instead of eating one another. When the animals are all friendly, it will be fun to have a lion for a pet, won't it? — That is going to happen in Paradise.

Do you know what Paradise is? — A Paradise

is a beautiful garden or park. It is a place of peace and pleasure.

God gave the first man, Adam, and his wife a Paradise in which to live. It was called the Garden of Eden. There were animals in that garden. But none of them hurt the others. There were also trees with lots of delicious fruit on them. And there was a river. It was a wonderful place to live.

But Adam and Eve lost that Paradise. They disobeyed God, so they could not live in Paradise anymore. There is no Garden of Eden now. So, what chance do we have to live in Paradise? —

Well, before he died on the torture stake, the Great Teacher talked about a new Paradise. A man had just said to him: "Jesus, remember me when you get into your kingdom." Jesus answered: "Truly I tell you today, You will be with me in Paradise."—Luke 23:42, 43.

Jesus did not say that they were going to be in Paradise that very same day. Both of them died and were buried on that day. But Jesus was talking about what would happen after he 'got into his kingdom.' Then there will be a Paradise again. The new Paradise will last forever.

Where will that Paradise be? — The first Paradise was right here on earth, wasn't it? So the new Paradise will be here on earth too. That is why Jesus taught us to pray for God's will to be done on earth. When that time comes, the whole earth will become a Paradise.

In Paradise there will be big changes made. The air will be clean and fresh and good to breathe. Water in the rivers will be clear and good. The land will grow plenty of food so that no one goes hungry. The whole earth will become like a park. It will be alive with birds and animals, trees and flowers of every kind.

But the biggest changes will be in the people. It is people who make a mess of the earth, isn't it? — Some of them live in messy homes. And they throw trash everywhere they go. But Paradise won't be like that. It will be a clean and pleasant place to live. So, if we want to live in Paradise, wouldn't you say that now is the time to learn to keep things neat and clean? — That's one way to show that we really want the earth to be a Paradise, isn't it? —

People will change in other ways too. Paradise

will be a place of peace. But not everyone today is peaceful. Some people scream at others. They hit and hurt other people. They act just like wild animals. They need to learn to live in peace. In Paradise, they "will not do any harm or cause any ruin."—Isaiah 11:9.

Are you always peaceful with others? — If we are going to live in Paradise, we need to learn to be peaceful, don't we? —

It will be a wonderful thing to live in Paradise. God promises that he will do marvelous things for us then. Open your Bible to Revelation chapter 21, verses 3 and 4, and let's read what it says: "Look! The tent of God is with mankind, and he will reside with them, and they will be his peoples. And God himself will be with them. And he will wipe out every tear from their eyes, and death will be no more, neither will mourning nor outcry nor pain be any more. The former things have passed away."

Just think about that! God will watch over us. We will never have to cry because we are unhappy. No one will have pain because he is sick. And no one will have to die. That is what it will be like in Paradise.

Do you really want to live in Paradise? — I do. What we do every day now has an effect on whether we will be there. If we want to live in Paradise, now is the time to prepare for it.

(This earth will last forever and God will make it a wonderful place to live. Read more about this at Psalms 104:5 [103:5, Dy]; 37:10, 11 [36:10, 11, Dy]; Proverbs 2:21, 22; Isaiah 35:5, 6; Micah 4:3, 4.)

45

How to Tell God, 'I Love You'

DID you know that someone loved you even before you were born? — Well, you see we knew you were coming. Of course, we didn't know what you would look like then. You were still growing inside your mother. But already your father and your mother were doing many things to show they loved you.

That's why there were clothes for you to wear as soon as you were born. And there was a little bed for you to sleep in.

And, my, how happy your father and mother were when they finally saw you! They loved you then. And they love you now, very, very much. You love your father and mother, too, don't you? —

But now I am thinking of someone else who also loved you before you were born. Do you know who? — It is Jehovah God. In fact, God loved all of us before we were born. Do you know how we know he did? —

Because a long time ago God sent his Son to give his life for us. Also, God is going to make the earth a beautiful garden where we can live forever in happiness, if we really want to.

How does this make you feel toward God? —
It makes me love him very, very much. I want to
serve him all my life. Do you? —

But how can we tell God that? — Jesus knew
just how to tell God that. Listen while I tell you
what he did.

One day he went to the Jordan River. John
the Baptist was there. Jesus and John waded out
into the water. The water was all the way up to
their waists. Do you have any idea of what they
were going to do? —

The man put one of his arms around behind
Jesus' shoulders. He put Jesus all the way under

the water for just a
second and then lifted
him out again. He
baptized him. Why
did he do that? Jesus
asked the man to do
it. But why? Do you
know? —

Jesus did it so that
God would know that Jesus wanted to serve
him all his life, yes, forever. But did God want
Jesus to be put under the water that way? —
Yes, he did. How do we know? —

Because when Jesus came up out of the water
he heard a big voice from heaven say: 'You
are my Son whom I love. I am very pleased with
you.'—Mark 1:9-11.

What did Jesus do after this? — Well, he

started going around talking about God to everyone who would listen. He told them about God's kingdom. He told them how they could live forever.

Some of the men and women believed what the Great Teacher taught them. But they felt sad. Do you know why? —

Because they thought of many bad things they had done. They knew that God was not pleased with those things. They knew the Bible said those things were wrong. Now they wanted to be like Jesus and please God. So, do you know what they did? —

They asked to be baptized just as Jesus had been baptized. They wanted to tell God that they loved him and that they wanted to serve him all their life.

We can do the same thing today. Of course, you are still growing up now. But you aren't going to spend your whole life just growing up, are you? — Of course not. Someday you'll be grown up. What are you going to do then? —

Will you be like Jesus? — Will you do what the men and women who believed in Jesus did? Will you get baptized? — If you do, you will be telling God that you love him. You will be telling him that you want to serve him all your life. I certainly hope you do that. And God will be very pleased if you do.

When a person is grown up, there are many things that he can do. Some people who are grown up live with their families. They work and earn money, and they buy things for their families. They buy clothes, food, furniture, even automobiles. This is nice. But is this the way to tell God that they love him? Is this the way to tell God that they want to serve him all their life? —

Many of these people do not even want to listen when another person tries to talk to them about the Bible. They may not even read the Bible. Some of them hardly ever talk about God or the Great Teacher, not even to their children. Some of them may not even thank God for the food they eat, or talk to him in prayer at night. They do not really love God, do they? — You wouldn't want to grow up and be like them, would you? — How sad that would be.

The Great Teacher talked about God to all sorts of people, including little children. He enjoyed talking about God and about the good things God will do for those who love him. He really meant it when he told God: 'Father, I love you and I want to serve you forever.' Learn all you can about the Great Teacher now while you're young. Let your heart get filled with love for Jehovah God. Then you, too, will really mean it when you tell God: 'I love you and I want to serve you forever.'

(Other texts you may read that show how we can prove our love for God are: Matthew 6:24-33; 24:14; 1 John 2:15-17; 5:3.)

46

The Way to Live Forever

JEHOVAH has given us many wonderful gifts. One of his finest gifts to us is life. Without it we could not do anything, could we? — But if we want to keep that gift, there are some things that we must do.

You are doing one of those things right now. So am I. We do it all day and all night, even when we are asleep. If we were to stop, we would die right away. Do you know what it is? — Yes, we are breathing.

There are other things that we do every day to keep alive. Can you name some of them? — We eat food. We drink water. And we sleep. God made us so that we cannot live without these things.

None of them are hard to do. In fact, I like eating. Don't you? — But how does food keep us alive? Do you know? What happens to it after we swallow it? —

Our body breaks the food into very tiny pieces. Then the blood carries these to every part of our body. This food is used in a marvelous way to build new bone, new flesh, new hair, nails, eyes and other body parts. Did you know that? —

You may wonder what happens to the old

187

body parts. These die off a little bit at a time and are taken away as wastes. The new ones take their place.

These changes are happening everywhere in our body. It does not take very long until our whole body is made over. Jehovah made our body so that it does this. He made it so that it would go on doing it forever. Yes, he made man to live forever.

But people die. Why? — Because Adam sinned against God. And we got sin from Adam. He spoiled man's good relationship with God. And our life depends on God.

To live forever, we need more than air and water and food and sleep. We need to have the right standing with God.

There is no doctor that can make us live forever. There is no magic pill that will keep us from dying. The only way we can live forever is by drawing close to God. The Great Teacher tells us how to do that.

Let's get our Bibles and open them to John chapter 17, verse 3. Here we find what Jesus said: "This means everlasting life, their taking in knowledge of you, the only true God, and of the one whom you sent forth, Jesus Christ."

What did the Great Teacher say that we need in order to live forever? — We need to take in knowledge. That means we need to learn. That is why we study the Bible.

But how will learning about Jehovah help us

to live forever? — Remember, all life comes from him. To have his favor, we must worship him as the only true God. But we cannot worship him in the right way unless we listen to what he says. Just as we need food every day, so we need to learn about Jehovah every day. This keeps us close to him. The Bible says: 'Man must live, not on bread alone, but on all the words that come from Jehovah's mouth.'—Matthew 4:4.

We also need to take in knowledge about someone besides God. Who is that? — Jesus Christ. This is because God sent Jesus to take away sin. He can take away the harm that Adam did when Adam sinned against God. Jesus can help us to get back into a good relationship with God. And that is not possible in any other way.

That is why the Bible says: "There is no salvation in anyone else." We have to learn about Jesus if we want to live forever. And if we really do have faith in him, we will be able to live forever. When he

189

brings good conditions to all the earth, he will help us to live forever and be happy. It is a sure thing. That is why the Bible says: "He that exercises faith in the Son has everlasting life." —Acts 4:12; John 3:36.

Now, what does it mean to 'exercise faith' in Jesus? — It means that we really believe that we cannot stay alive without him. We believe that God gives us everlasting life through Jesus. Do you believe that? —

'Exercising faith' in Jesus means something else too. It means that we believe him so much that we do what he says. We do not do just some things and not others. We do all the things he says. And we do them because we really want to. Is that what you want to do? —

One of the things that the Great Teacher tells us to do is to talk to other people about God and his kingdom. He did it himself to show us how. So, if we have really learned from Jesus, that is something that we will do. Do you do that? —

But that is not all that counts. Every day we should do the things that the Bible says are right. We must be careful not to do bad things. We should show that we truly love one another.

If we do these things, it shows that we have really been listening to the Great Teacher.

(True disciples of Jesus Christ will really be able to live forever in happiness right on this earth. Read what the Bible says about this at Psalm 37:29, 34 [36:29, 34, Dy], Matthew 19:16-21 and Romans 6:23.)

Other Aids for Your Family

Would you like other valuable aids for your family? You may obtain either one of the following by writing to Watch Tower, using the appropriate address on the next page.

● **Making Your Family Life Happy.** A splendid aid for finding the key to family happiness. Discussed herein is every aspect of marriage, laying a fine foundation for it, the roles of husband and wife, the rearing of children and building as a family for life everlasting. Delightfully illustrated, hardbound, pocket-size, 192 pages.

● **Questions Young People Ask —Answers That Work.** This book will help teenagers to counteract the immoral influences of today's world. Dishonesty, alcohol and drug abuse, sexual morality, dating and courtship are some of the subjects under discussion. Hardbound, 320 pages.

Would you welcome more information or a free home Bible study?

Write Watch Tower at appropriate address below.

ALASKA 99507: 2552 East 48th Ave., Anchorage. **ALBANIA:** Kutia Postare 3, Tiranë. **ARGENTINA:** Elcano 3820, 1427 Buenos Aires. **AUSTRALIA:** Box 280, Ingleburn, N.S.W. 2565. **AUSTRIA:** Postfach 67, A-1134 Vienna [13 Gallgasse 42–44, Vienna]. **BAHAMAS:** Box N-1247, Nassau, N.P. **BARBADOS:** Fontabelle Rd., Bridgetown. **BELGIUM:** rue d'Argile–Potaardestraat 60, B-1950 Kraainem. **BELIZE:** Box 257, Belize City. **BENIN, REP. OF:** BP 06-1131, Cotonou. **BOLIVIA:** Casilla No. 1440, La Paz. **BRAZIL:** Caixa Postal 92, 18270-970 Tatuí, SP. **BULGARIA:** P.K. 353, Sofia 1000. **CANADA:** Box 4100, Halton Hills (Georgetown), Ontario L7G 4Y4. **CENTRAL AFRICAN REPUBLIC:** B.P. 662, Bangui. **CHILE:** Casilla 267, Puente Alto [Av. Concha y Toro 3456, Puente Alto]. **COLOMBIA:** Apartado Aéreo 85058, Bogotá 1, D.E. **COSTA RICA:** Apartado 10043, San José. **CÔTE D'IVOIRE (IVORY COAST), WEST AFRICA:** 06 B P 393, Abidjan 06. **CROATIA:** p.p. 417, 41001 Zagreb. **CYPRUS:** P. O. Box 33, Dhali, Nicosia. **CZECH REPUBLIC:** P.O. Box 90, 198 00 Praha 9. **DENMARK:** Stenhusvej 28, DK-4300 Holbæk. **DOMINICAN REPUBLIC:** Apartado 1742, Santo Domingo. **ECUADOR:** Casilla 09-01-4512, Guayaquil. **EL SALVADOR:** Apartado Postal 401, San Salvador. **ENGLAND:** The Ridgeway, London NW7 1RP. **FIJI:** Box 23, Suva. **FINLAND:** Postbok 68, FIN-01301 Vantaa 30. **FRANCE:** B.P. 63, F-92105 Boulogne-Billancourt Cedex. **FRENCH GUIANA:** 15 rue Chawari, Cogneau Larivot, 97351 Matoury. **GERMANY:** Niederselters, Am Steinfels, D-65618 Selters. **GHANA:** Box 760, Accra. **GREECE:** P.O. Box 112, GR-322 00 Thiva. **GUADELOUPE:** Monmain, 97180 Sainte Anne. **GUAM 96913:** 143 Jehovah St., Barrigada. **GUATEMALA:** 17 Calle 13-63, Zona 11, 01011 Guatemala. **GUYANA:** 50 Brickdam, Georgetown 16. **HAITI:** Post Box 185, Port-au-Prince. **HAWAII 96819:** 2055 Kam IV Rd., Honolulu. **HONDURAS:** Apartado 147, Tegucigalpa. **HONG KONG:** 4 Kent Road, Kowloon Tong. **HUNGARY:** Pf. 223, H-1425 Budapest. **ICELAND:** P. O. Box 8496, IS-128 Reykjavik. **INDIA:** Post Bag 10, Lonavla, Pune Dis., Mah. 410 401. **IRELAND:** 29A Jamestown Road, Finglas, Dublin 11. **ISRAEL:** P. O. Box 961, 61-009 Tel Aviv. **ITALY:** Via della Bufalotta 1281, I-00138 Rome RM. **JAMAICA:** Box 180, Kingston 10. **JAPAN:** 1271 Nakashinden, Ebina City, Kanagawa Pref., 243-04. **KENYA:** Box 47788, Nairobi. **KOREA, REPUBLIC OF:** Box 33 Pyungtaek P. O., Kyunggido, 450-600. **LEEWARD ISLANDS:** Box 119, St. Johns, Antigua. **LIBERIA:** P. O. Box 10-0380, 1000 Monrovia 10. **LUXEMBOURG:** B. P. 2186, L-1021 Luxembourg, G. D. **MADAGASCAR:** B. P. 511, Antananarivo 101. **MALAYSIA:** 28 Jalan Kampar, Off Jalan Landasan, 41300 Klang, Sel. **MARTINIQUE:** Cours Campeche, Morne Tartenson, 97200 Fort de France. **MAURITIUS:** Clairfond No. 2, Box 54, Vacoas. **MEXICO:** Apartado Postal 896, 06002 Mexico, D. F. **MOZAMBIQUE:** Caixa Postal 2600, Maputo. **MYANMAR:** P.O. Box 62, Yangon. **NETHERLANDS:** Noordbargerstraat 77, NL-7812 AA Emmen. **NETHERLANDS ANTILLES:** P.O. Box 4708, Willemstad, Curaçao. **NEW CALEDONIA:** B.P. 787, Nouméa. **NEW ZEALAND:** P.O. Box 142, Manurewa. **NICARAGUA:** Apartado 3587, Managua. **NIGERIA:** P.M.B. 1090, Benin City, Edo State. **NORWAY:** Gaupeveien 24, N-1914 Ytre Enebakk. **PAKISTAN:** 197-A Ahmad Block, New Garden Town, Lahore 54600. **PANAMA:** Apartado 6-2671, Zona 6A, El Dorado. **PAPUA NEW GUINEA:** Box 636, Boroko, N.C.D. **PARAGUAY:** Díaz de Solís 1485 esq. C.A. López, Sajonia, Asunción. **PERU:** Apartado 18-1055, Lima 18 [Av. El Cortijo 329, Monterrico Chico, Lima 33]. **PHILIPPINES, REPUBLIC OF:** P. O. Box 2044, 1099 Manila [186 Roosevelt Ave., San Francisco del Monte, 1105 Quezon City]. **POLAND:** Skr. Poczt. 13, PL-05-830 Nadarzyn. **PORTUGAL:** Apartado 91, P-2766 Estoril Codex [Rua Conde Barão, 511, Alcabideche, P-2765 Estoril]. **PUERTO RICO 00970:** P.O. Box 3980, Guaynabo. **ROMANIA:** Str. Parfumului 22, RO-74121, Bucharest. **RUSSIA:** ul. Tankistov, 4, Solnechnoye, Sestroretzky Rayon, 189640 St. Petersburg. **SENEGAL:** B.P. 3107, Dakar. **SIERRA LEONE, WEST AFRICA:** P. O. Box 136, Freetown. **SLOVAKIA:** P. O. Box 17, 810 00 Bratislava 1. **SLOVENIA:** Poljanska cesta 77a, SLO-61000 Ljubljana. **SOLOMON ISLANDS:** P.O. Box 166, Honiara. **SOUTH AFRICA:** Private Bag X2067, Krugersdorp, 1740. **SPAIN:** Apartado postal 132, E-28850 Torrejón de Ardoz (Madrid). **SRI LANKA, REP. OF:** 62 Layard's Road, Colombo 5. **SURINAME:** P.O. Box 49, Paramaribo. **SWEDEN:** Box 5, S-732 21 Arboga. **SWITZERLAND:** P.O. Box 225, CH-3602 Thun [Ulmenweg 45, Thun]. **TAHITI:** B.P. 518, Papeete. **TAIWAN:** 107 Yun Ho Street, Taipei 10613. **THAILAND:** 69/1 Soi Phasuk, Sukhumvit Rd., Soi 2, Bangkok 10110. **TOGO:** B.P. 4460, Lome. **TRINIDAD AND TOBAGO, REP. OF:** Lower Rapsey Street & Laxmi Lane, Curepe. **UKRAINE:** Glavposhtamt Box 246, 290000 Lviv. **UNITED STATES OF AMERICA:** 25 Columbia Heights, Brooklyn, NY 11201-2483. **URUGUAY:** Francisco Bauzá 3372, 11600 Montevideo. **VENEZUELA:** Apartado 20.364, Caracas, DF 1020A [Av. La Victoria; cruce con 17 de diciembre, La Victoria, Edo. Aragua 2121A]. **WESTERN SAMOA:** P. O. Box 673, Apia. **YUGOSLAVIA, F.R.:** Milorada Mitrovića 4, YU-11 000 Belgrade. **ZAIRE REP. OF:** B.P. 634, Limete, Kinshasa. **ZAMBIA:** Box 33459, Lusaka 10101. **ZIMBABWE:** 35 Fife Avenue, Harare.